More Stories to Enlighten

A Continuing Collection of Legends, Modern Parables and Personal Stories used to Illuminate the Lectionary

Written, collected and compiled by
The Rev. Dee Ann de Montmollin

College State of Mind
Publisher

Also published by The Rev. Dee Ann de Montmollin:
Stories to Enlighten

FIRST U.S. EDITION 2016

Published in the United States by College State of Mind, LLC

10 9 8 7 6 5 4 3 2 1
PRINTED IN THE UNITED STATES

PREFACE

To all the story-tellers of the world, my sincere gratitude. Lives are richer because of you.

Everyone loves a good story. We know the Old Testament was passed on by stories, the oral tradition. And the people listened.

Jesus told parables to help the disciples and others better understand what he was saying. And they listened.

Over the years, we have told our children the fairy tales and other stories that we heard as we were growing up. And they listened. And they will tell their children. And they will listen.

Over the last fifteen years, I have frequently used stories in my sermons to help better relate the scriptures to our world today. And for the most part, the people listened.

I thank all the parishioners who have listened to the wonder of God's love as told through the scriptures. Each of you made a difference in my life: through your devotion, through your empathy, through your laughter, through your tears. But mostly through your presence.

I have found that people not only remember the stories, but respond to them through their actions and through their relationships with others. They, too, have helped show the love of God.

As with most legends and stories, the original sources of some of these stories have long been forgotten. Where I have been able, I have attributed the story to an individual story-teller. To those of you I may have missed, sorry and thank you.

My greatest joy in life is to help show the love of God to others. Especially to those who are lonely, discouraged, or despondent. My prayer is that something in one of these stories will bring you closer to God and to the joy of helping others.

God has given each of us an incredible gift, but we must always remember that a gift is not a gift until it is received. I hope that you receive and use the gift of these stories to deepen your relationship with others and with God. I encourage you to keep your Bible at hand as you read the stories, so that you can read and refer back to the related scriptures at the same time.

I thank God for each of you. I thank God for my family and those families who have included me as a member of their family. But mostly, I thank God for allowing me to serve you as an Episcopal priest.

The Christ in me salutes the Christ in you!

Exodus 20:1–17
A Guide for Living

It seems that Moses wasn't feeling well and he was very upset. He decided he would go up on the mountain and see God.

"You know my life has not been easy, God. First my mother put me in a basket and floated me down a river," Moses said. "Then there was Pharaoh and the Red Sea. Then I was in the wilderness with all these complaining Israelites . . . You remember the burning bush, the plagues, and then the Passover."

God said "Yes, Moses, I do remember."

"There's a lot more," Moses continued. "You remember everything, so I don't have to tell you the rest. But I really can't handle much more, and I have this splitting headache."

God looked at Moses and said, "Here, take these two tablets. They should help."

The two tablets did help because they were the Ten Commandments and they were designed to help humanity, not by putting us in a moral strait jacket, but by providing us with positive boundaries to guide our behavior.

If a river has no boundaries, it becomes a stagnant swamp. Boundaries give us the ability to function in an optimum way. We need to know the Ten Commandments, and we need to use them as a guide for living.

Mark 1:9-15

Lead Me Not Into Temptation

In C. S. Lewis' book, *The Lion, The Witch and the Wardrobe,* the wicked queen entices the boy, Edmund, with a box of enchanted Turkish Delights. Each piece is sweet and delicious, and Edmund has never tasted anything better. There is only one problem. The more he eats of the enchanted Turkish Delights, the more he wants.

He doesn't know that this is the wicked queen's plan. The more he eats, the more he will want, and thus he will eat and eat until it kills him. It would never satisfy his hunger; it would never fill him up . . . it would simply kill him. That's the danger of the evil of temptation. It eventually kills.

We don't like to admit it but there are times when all of us are tempted. No one of us ever escapes from some form of temptation. Some of us are tempted more than others.

Temptation. No one of us is too old or too young, too sophisticated or too naive, to escape the tempter. Temptation can lead us into all kinds of problems.

Luke 13:22–35

She Died So That Her Chicks Could Live

God is like the mother hen who will protect her chicks until death. We hear Jesus say, *"How often have I desired to gather your children together as a hen gathers her brood under her wings, and you were not willing."*

These words remind me of twin hippopotami born in a zoo a few years ago. A local celebrity was asked to name the two babies. The only hitch was that the mother hippo wouldn't let anyone close enough to determine whether the babies were male or female. The two babies paddled or walked just under their mother and no one wanted to upset the two-ton hippo mother. Mother hippos can get very agitated if there is any threat to their babies and no one was prepared to risk tangling with an upset hippo. The baby hippos were protected by their hippo mother who provided for them just what they needed. They remained nameless for a year.

Chickens don't stray far from the mother hen for they know that there is no better place than their mother's wings for protection. Their mother provides food, protection, warmth and nurture.

There was a forest fire in Yellowstone National Park several years ago and rangers found an ashy, ossified bird at the foot of a tree. Sickened, they gently prodded it with a stick and three little chicks scrambled from under the mother bird's wings. They hypothesized that the mother bird had carried her offspring to the base of the tree, gathering them under her wings, instinctively aware that toxic smoke would rise. She could have flown away, but she would not abandon her chicks for her own safety.

Even as she burned, she protected them, unwaveringly. Mama Bird was willing to die, so that her chicks under the cover of her wings would live.

It is like that throughout the animal world whether you are talking about hippos, kittens, chickens or puppies. It seems that the young have sense enough to stay close to their nurturing parent. This is what is supposed to happen with humankind. God created families so that the young, the offspring could be nurtured and protected.

It seems like when it comes to God, our heavenly parent, it's another story. We exhibit unnatural behavior by turning away from the love and protection of the God who created us.

When we hear the words, *"Jerusalem, Jerusalem, how often have I desired to gather your children together and you were not willing,"* God is speaking to us saying our name . . . *"how often have I desired to gather you, to put my arms around you, to protect you, and you were not willing."* He is speaking to each of us.

Life is like a Puzzle

In a writing class for senior citizens, 98-year-old Jessie Lee Brown Foveaux wrote her advice about facing hard times. The publishing rights for the book *Any Given Day* was sold for one million dollars.

Jessie Lee wrote:

"You say you think life is like a big puzzle. How right you are, my dear. Life is like a puzzle, and the pieces fall into place each day, and the giant puzzle lasts all along life's way.

"But, God will, if we ask him, give us the strength for whatever may come, so let's put guilt and confusion behind us.

"Once we ask and are forgiven, we can start the new day with joy and accept the fact that we are all sinners saved by God's grace.

"Then we can have a cheerful smile to light up our face to greet anyone we may meet anytime or anyplace."

Eluding His Rescue

There is a story of California police who were staging an intense search for a Volkswagen that was stolen, even to the point of placing announcements on local radio stations to contact the thief.

The reason for the intensity of the search lay on the front seat of the stolen car - a box containing crackers that, unknown to the thief, were laced with poison. The car owner had created the poisonous crackers intending to use them as rat bait.

Now the police and even the owner of the VW Bug were more interested in apprehending the thief to save his life than to recover the car.

So often when we run from God, we feel it is to escape his punishment. But what we are actually doing is eluding his rescue.

Let Us Remember, Always

Four years ago I said the following to my congregation:

"This past week, I knew the love of God over and over again. On Monday, our daughter-in-law had an emergency c/section for the delivery of our twin grandchildren, Cali and Colby. While we were waiting, I found the chapel. We were at St. Joseph's Women's Hospital, so of course, there was a chapel.

"I pleaded with God to take care of those babies.

"They were born and our little boy, Colby, developed some breathing problems and went into Neonatal ICU. Our little girl, though only a bit over four pounds, was doing well and spent her time with her mommy and daddy in the hospital room. She was going to go home but now is also with her brother in NICU at St. Joseph's.

"And what do we do now during this time? We pray. And we trust in God's love.

"I know that there will be many times that our trust in God will be tested over the years with these children, as it is with all our children. But I also know that God loves them more than we can possibly imagine – more than all the stars in the sky and the all the grains of sand on all the beaches."

More recently I told them:

"This past Thursday marked the fourth birthday for the twins. Even though their official party will be soon, we celebrated not only their lives but the love of God in their lives.

"No one of us can tell what tomorrow brings, so what we do today is offer our love to each and every person we meet.

"Make your life one long gift to others. It is what our Savior did for us. It is what we are called to do for others.

We are to give God our best, for that is what he gave to us – his Son.

"God wants our love, no excuses. If our love is guided by what is true and good then we will choose God and love him above all else. God certainly loved us.

"God so loved us so much that he gave his son. Let us always remember the time of Christ on the cross. Always."

It's What Happens
In You That Counts

Many years ago Protestant minister Harry Emerson Fosdick told of a teenage girl stricken with polio.

One of her friends had once told her that, "Affliction does so color life."

To which this courageous girl agreed, but said "Yes, but I can choose which color my life will be."

She had discovered one of life's great secrets. It's not what happens *to* you, but what happens *in* you that counts.

What Do We Do About Our Past?

Two men were drinking coffee and taking a break from their daily work. One said to the other, "Say, you look depressed. What are you thinking about?"

"My future," his friend sighed.

"What makes your future look so hopeless?" the first man asked.

"My past," he replied.

The apostle Paul understood the corrosive power of regret. As a devoted Pharisee, Paul - then called Saul - had been a chief persecutor of the early Christian believers. He approved of the stoning of Stephen.

Even after his name was changed to Paul and he tried to join up with the other Christians, they rejected him at first. They knew of his past. Eventually, however, Paul became the most effective Christian evangelist in history.

Even though Paul knew the power of regrets, he also knew the indisputable power of Christ to change a person from the inside out. He knew the power that changed a man from a murderer to a minister.

Paul told the people that Jesus didn't come to make bad people good. He came to give dead people life. This is not resurrection from the dead like Lazarus; but resurrection of our spiritual lives.

Paul is not reminding the Ephesian believers of their past to cause them shame.

So what do we do with our past? What do we do with our fears and failings and foolish decisions?

Paul tells us: *"It is by grace you have been saved. For we are what he has made us, created in Christ Jesus for good works, which God prepared beforehand to be our way of life."*

Getting His Act Together

A young man was having trouble getting his act together, and decided to take out his frustrations on God. He shook his fist at the heavens and said, "What a terrible world this is! Even I could make a better world than this one!" And then, from somewhere deep inside, he heard God's answer: "That's what you're supposed to do."

Let Us Learn From the Children

To teach us about greatness and the kingdom of Heaven, Jesus wants us to learn from the children.

There are certain qualities in children that we should recognize and acknowledge. Jesus himself possesses these qualities, qualities for us to know and to have and to live out as Christians. Here are seven of these qualities:

1. Children are frank and honest.

2. Children do not hide what they are feeling, until we in society teach them to do so.

3. Children look for nurturing and for the community of others.

4. Another quality in children is that they are idealistic.

5. Children love to serve others and they do it with enthusiasm.

6. Children are kind and generous.

Read how many of these qualities are demonstrated in this warm story:

A number of years ago, a 10-year-old boy walked up to the counter of a soda shop and climbed onto a stool. He caught the eye of the waitress and asked, "How much is an ice cream sundae?"

"Fifty cents," the waitress replied.

The boy reached into his pockets, pulled out a handful of change, and began counting. The waitress frowned impatiently. After all, she had other customers waiting.

The boy squinted up at the waitress. "How much is one scoop of just plain ice cream?"

The waitress sighed and rolled her eyes. "Thirty-five cents," she said with a sigh of irritation.

Again the boy counted his coins. At last, he said, "I'll have one scoop of plain vanilla ice cream, please." The waitress took the thirty-five cents, brought the ice cream, and walked away.

About 10 minutes later, she returned and found the ice cream dish empty. The boy was gone. She picked up the empty dish and swallowed hard.

There on the counter, next to the wet spot where the ice cream dish had been, were two nickels and five pennies. The boy had had enough for a sundae, but he ordered one scoop of just plain ice cream so he could leave a tip.

7. And finally, the way a child depends on their parents for their well-being is the same way we should relate to God. Our relationship with God is that of a child to a loving parent. We are completely dependent on God's love and what Jesus has done for us through his death and resurrection.

Let us learn from the lessons of children. Let us be like the children: frank, honest, innocent and idealistic. Serve others and understand the connection we need with others.

Praise Him and Highly Exalt Him Forever

Several years ago, I was at Sea Island, South Carolina for a personal spiritual retreat. The first evening of my retreat, I went on a walk by myself and was looking into the ocean and realized that there were at least five dolphin swimming close by. I started talking to them and splashing the water and telling them how beautiful they were. Within minutes they were flipping and fanning their tails. I counted eight of them. Before I left, two of them put their heads out of the water and looked at me with their beautiful smiling faces.

I encouraged Phil to come with me the next morning and there they were again . . . the more we applauded and talked with them, the more they stayed with us, even swimming as close as ten feet away! It was though they appreciated the attention

Every walk on the beach reminded me of the Song of Creation (BCP, p.88).

Glorify the Lord, O springs of water, seas, and streams,
O Whales and all that move in the waters,
All birds of the air, glorify the Lord,
Praise him and highly exalt him forever.

Through this 'encounter' with the dolphin, I realized once again how important it is to let others know how much we appreciate them . . . and appreciate Him!

Exodus 20:1-17
Wouldn't That Be Something!

The Commandments are not intended to teach us about rules but about our relationship with God.

A monk wrote these words almost 1000 years ago: "When I was a young man, I wanted to change the world. I found it was difficult to change the world, so I tried to change my nation. When I found I couldn't change the nation I began to focus on my town. I couldn't change the town and as an older man I tried to change my family. Now as an old man, I realize the only thing I can change is myself and suddenly I realize that if long ago I had changed myself I could have made an impact on my family. My family and I could have made an impact on our town. Their impact could have changed the nation and I could indeed have changed the world."

That is why God gave these Ten Commandments. If we love God, our creator, we will live them. If you live the commandments, you will be changed. And who knows . . . perhaps with that change, our world would be changed!

Wouldn't that be something!

Our Whole Selves Will Follow

During our walk on the Camino de Santiago, we started singing songs. One group member loved some of the Peter, Paul and Mary songs. That reminded me of Paul Stoke, the second member of the folk singing trio.

Paul was going through a time of searching and crisis. He was disturbed by the hypocrisy in his life. He turned to an old friend, Bob Dylan, for advice.

Two things that Dylan said stood out in Paul's mind: One, go for a long walk in the country, and two, read the Bible.

What great advice to give to anyone! Paul took the advice. He walked in the country, and it helped him sort out his priorities. And he read the Bible. Although his folk group had sung several spirituals and gospel tunes, Paul had never opened a Bible before. But now he read through the entire New Testament and parts of the Old.

He had a hard time with some of it - it was slow and often mysterious. But something real happened in Paul's life during that time. He decided to live his life not for himself, not for others - but for Jesus.

I wonder what would happen if we would take more walks and read the Bible every day? We would probably become like the high jumper who set a world record. When asked how he did this high jump, he said he threw his heart over the bar and the rest of him followed.

To be truly like Jesus, you and I are to throw our hearts over the altar, so that our whole selves will follow.

By the way, do you know which three people in the Bible flew on a jet plane? (The answer can be found above.)

Matthew 25:31–46

A Perfect Response

When Rudyard Kipling was at the height of his popularity as a writer, it was said of him "that every word he wrote was worth 25 shillings."

Some college students at Oxford got wind of this and (you know how college students sometimes are) they wrote Kipling a letter which read like this:

"Dear Mr. Kipling, We understand that every word you write is worth 25 shillings. Enclosed are 25 shillings. Please send us your best word!"

Kipling rose to the occasion and sent back the perfect response, a one-word telegram which read: "THANKS!"

The Power of Prayer

I remember when my friend Ann Rose called me that day. She had just been informed that her sister Dale had been in a terrible automobile accident earlier in the day. Ann lives in Miami; Dale in Jacksonville, 350 miles away.

All Ann knew at the time was that that her sister had at least fourteen places on her body that were broken. Her whole left side of her body including a shattered hip, leg and ankle. Her clavicle, her ribs were fractured, and her right arm and hand were broken.

I immediately told Ann I would go to the church, light a candle, and pray. Ann and I prayed together for Dale on the phone that day and every day for months after. Dale ended up on many church prayer lists.

But the incredible thing is what happened at the time of the accident. When the truck jumped the median and hit her car, many people began to stop to see what happened. Of course, 911 was called.

A truck driver who was driving behind her stopped, looked in the driver's window and saw that she was breathing even though she was unconscious. He noticed that the seat belt was tightened around her neck and was strangling her. So he broke the window and cut the seat belt with his pocket knife. When he did this, he noticed that she was wearing a cross.

By now many people were there. There was nothing they thought they could do until the jaws-of-life equipment could get there to free her from the mangled car. But there was something they could do. These people began to encircle the car, reaching out to lay their hands on the car, and prayed for Dale.

Dale was taken to the trauma hospital and immediately operated on. There were no contacts to call right away because her purse with her cell phone had been knocked out of sight in the car. In the rescue helicopter Dale came to long enough to mumble the phone number of her closest friend, and it was through the contact with the friend that Dale's husband was reached.

A woman at the scene of the accident followed the ambulance to the hospital and waited to see if Dale survived. She was the one to tell Dale's husband and children about the people surrounding the car and praying for Dale inside while the jaws-of-life and rescue helicopter were on the way. While Dale suffered many, many broken bones, the doctor could not believe she did not have any neurological injuries. No internal organs were effected.

As Dale later reflected about this, she realized that the prayers of these unknown people who stopped, held hands, touched the car, and prayed, were the prayers that sustained her through surgery.

Dale is fortunate she is alive. She went through six months of not being able to use her arms and learning how to walk again. She was determined to walk down the aisle at her daughter's wedding; and she did. Today she continues to teach art to her students. Dale knows the power of touch and the power of prayer of those persons even though she does not know their names.

One prayer that sustained her through all her rehab was the prayer on page 461 of the Book of Common Prayer:

This is another day O Lord, I know not what it brings forth but make me ready Lord for whatever it may be.

Dale later learned that the woman who followed her to the hospital was at the time trying to discern whether she had been called to be a Presbyterian minister. She said being at the scene of the accident had helped make her decision that she was going to become a minister.

Mark 6:1-13
Faith is More Than A Mere Intellectual Assent

Have you thought about what a leap of faith it was for Christopher Columbus to embark on his great adventure? He certainly exhibited perseverance and commitment to his dream.

It is said that the average speed of the Santa Maria during the voyage across the Atlantic was two miles an hour. Yet we get frustrated when we have to slow down to twenty in traffic. Perhaps that is why Columbus' crew became almost mutinous at times. Columbus must have been frustrated on such occasions with their lack of faith.

Many believe in the existence of God. But there are exceptions.

A cynical young medical student confronted his minister: "I have dissected the human body," he announced, "and I found no soul."

The minister said, "That's interesting. When you dissected the brain did you find a thought? When you dissected the eye did you find vision? When you dissected the heart did you find love?"

The student answered thoughtfully, "No, I did not."

The minister said gently, "Of course you believe in the existence of thoughts, of vision, and of love. The human soul is the totality of man's existence in relationship with God. Just because you cannot locate it on a medical chart does not mean that it does not exist."

Most people accept such reasoning. We believe with our heads, but that is not the kind of belief that faith in Christ is about. *"Even the demons believe,"* say the scriptures, *"and tremble."*

Faith in Christ is more than mere intellectual assent. It is believing with the heart, with the will, with adoration, and with action.

Harsh Criticism

No one has ever accomplished anything of note without critics. Certainly Jesus had his critics. In this lesson from Mark's Gospel, Jesus is still in the early part of his ministry. But almost immediately he runs into opposition. First of all, it was from his own family.

Mark tells us that when Jesus' family heard about what was happening, they went to take charge of him. Sometimes it is those closest to us who have the hardest time coming to grips with our dreams and aspirations.

Winston Churchill, truly a man of heroic stature, was one of the most criticized politicians who ever lived. But he knew how to handle his detractors.

Perhaps the most famous of Churchill's exchanges was one he had at a state dinner with Nancy Astor, the first woman to sit as a member of Parliament in the House of Commons.

Lady Astor had a reputation for acid wit and instant repartee. During this dinner Lady Astor was compelled to listen to Churchill expound his views on a great number of subjects, all of them at variance with her own strongly-held views.

Finally, no longer able to hold her tongue, she spat, "Winston, if you were my husband, I would flavor your coffee with poison."

To which Churchill immediately replied, "Madam, if I were your husband, I would gladly drink it."

In the Name of Christ

A father and son were walking down a busy New York City street on New Year's Eve. An unshaven dirty old beggar clutched the arm of the father and begged for money. The boy backed away in repulsiveness.

The father said, "Son, you shouldn't treat anyone like that!"

The boy replied, "Dad, he's nothing but a bum."

The father answered, "He is still a child of God." Taking money out of his wallet, the father told his son, "Give this to the man and tell him you are giving it in Jesus Christ's name."

Of course the boy did not want to do it but reluctantly went to the beggar and said, "Excuse me sir, I give you this money in the name of Christ."

In utter amazement, the beggar took off his hat and bowed graciously, and said, "And I thank you, young sir, in the name of Christ."

That lesson in life was the best New Year's present the father could have given his son.

Faith at Its Very Best

Are we like the old man walking down the road on a donkey while he carried a 200-pound sack of wheat on his shoulder? Someone asked him why he didn't take the weight off of his shoulders and strap it to the donkey. "Oh, no!" he protested. "I couldn't ask the donkey to carry all that weight."

Many of us are carrying burdens today that we do not have to carry. It is only the lack of faith, trust, and confidence that God really is alive and able to relieve us of our burdens that keeps us in bondage.

It would be far more desirable if we were like the young man who was in a marathon race. He was falling farther and farther behind the other runners. Suddenly it looked as if he were saying something to himself and then his legs began to move with a steadier stroke. He began to pick up speed. By the time he reached the finish line he had passed all of the others and had won the race.

Afterwards, when someone asked him what he was saying to himself as he was running, he replied, "Oh, I wasn't talking to myself. I was talking to God. I was saying, 'Lord, you pick them up and I'll put them down . . . You pick them up and I'll put them down . . . .' "

That's faith at its very best. Faith always moves forward. It is more than just believing with the head. It is a dynamic interaction with God's will and purpose. It is living with a positive expectation regardless of our circumstances. It is the conviction that because He lives, we can live joyfully, abundantly, fruitfully.

Count Your Blessings

A favorite *Peanuts* comic strip is the one that came out some years ago. Lucy is feeling sorry for herself and she laments, "My life is a drag. I'm completely fed up. I've never felt so low in my life."

Her little brother Linus tries to console her and he says, "Lucy, when you're in a mood like this, you should try to think of things you have to be thankful for; in other words, count your blessings."

To that, Lucy says, "Ha! That's a good one! I could count my blessings on one finger! I've never had anything and I never will have anything. I don't get half the breaks that other people do. Nothing ever goes right for me! And you talk about counting blessings! You talk about being thankful! What do I have to be thankful for?"

Linus says, "Well, for one thing, you have a little brother who loves you."

With that, Lucy runs and hugs her little brother Linus as she cries tears of joy. And while she's hugging him tightly, Linus says, "Every now and then, I say the right thing."

You see, we are all Lucy in the Peanuts cartoon. We forget to be grateful for our splendid lives. And we all have a little brother like Linus that loves us.

Be thankful for the people you love and who love you. Be thankful that God so loved the world that He gave His only Son.

Count your spiritual blessings. Focus on them and you will understand what real gratitude is all about.

Her Inheritance in Heaven

A few years ago, someone broke into the home of Christian author and evangelist Anne Graham Lots. The robbers took everything of value in the home and left Anne with a deep sense of fear and instability. The night after the break-in, Anne lay awake and contemplated her many fears. She started recalling scripture.

She realized that even if the robbers took everything of value from her, she still had an inheritance in heaven that could never be taken away. Suddenly, all her fear left her, and Anne fell asleep counting her blessings.

Here is the alphabetical list of blessings she came up with; twenty-six blessings in all. Anne realized she was: Accepted by God, Beloved by God, Chosen by God, Delivered by God, Enlightened by God, Forgiven by God.

She discovered she had the Grace of God, Hope for the future, Inheritance in heaven, Justification, Knowledge of God, Love, Mercy of God, Nearness to God, Oneness with God, Peace, Quickening of the Spirit.

She reminded herself she was Redeemed, Sealed with the Holy Spirit, Treasured by God, United with other believers, Validated as an authentic child of God.

She realized she had Wisdom; and one day she would be eXalted with God in Z-end.

Anne Graham Lotz knew that day that relationships matter. Relationships with one another and our relationship with God. The blessings we need to focus on are not physical or material, but emotional and spiritual.

Don't Sell That Cow

In a convent, the wise old Mother Superior was very ill. The nuns all gathered around the sick bed, trying to lift her spirits and make her as comfortable as possible. They offered her some fresh warm milk from one of the cows they kept in the barn, but she refused to drink it.

Then one of the young sisters remembered the unopened bottle of Irish whiskey in the kitchen cupboard. It was a Christmas present someone had given the chaplain. She took the glass of milk back to the kitchen and poured a generous amount of the Irish whiskey into the warm milk.

Back at Mother Superior's sickbed, she held the glass to the old nun's lips. Mother Superior drank a little, then a little more. Before they knew it, she had drunk the entire glass right down to the last drop.

"Reverend Mother," one the of the senior sisters in the convent asked, "is there anything else we can do for you now?" The old nun raised herself up out of bed, and with a glow on her face, pointed out the window in the direction of the barn, and exclaimed: "Whatever you do, don't ever sell that cow!"

It was the distilled 'spirits' that gave a burst of flavor to the milk and a blast of energy to old Mother Superior, just as it was the Holy Spirit who gave flavor and power and energy to the Church on Pentecost. Without the Holy Spirit, the Good News is stale, God is far away, Jesus stays in the past.

Spirit of Truth

The mission was called "Project Pearl." Its mission was to give Bibles to people in China. In 1981, Pastor Chen was arrested for his part in delivering more than one million Bibles to Swatow, on the south China coast. Two government investigators arrested Pastor Chen because he refused to release the names of those in charge of "Project Pearl."

They took Pastor Chen into a courtyard at the prison and made him stand on a tall wooden box. A rope was put around his neck and tightened. The rope was fixed on a wooden beam above him. The box he was standing on was about four feet high, and very narrow. The first investigator yelled, "We have given up on you. The moment you sway, or when your legs collapse from exhaustion, you will hang yourself. This is the penalty for your stubbornness."

The two investigators were assigned to keep watch on Chen. While he was hanging there, Chen began to witness about Jesus. "Have you ever heard about Jesus?"

"Quiet Christian!" spat the investigator. "We don't want to hear about your Jesus! It's just an old myth."

Chen told the investigators about how the love of Jesus was a healing, transforming, accepting love and that it was not myth but truth. The investigators only laughed.

The long hours soon became days, yet Chen had to remain still. His body cried for sleep, but he could not give in to his feelings. His legs developed terrible cramps, and in trying to relieve his legs by shaking them, he nearly hanged himself.

Soon he felt nothing in his legs, and they had swollen to twice their normal size. The only relief he received was the rain. He would stick his thickened tongue out to gain some moisture. Five days passed. Six. Seven. Still Chen had not toppled over and died. Eight days. Nine days.

The word of Chen living was going around the prison. Surely no man could survive this long. No food. No water. No sleep. It was impossible for him to still be alive. Ten days passed. Eleven, and then twelve.

On the thirteenth day, a huge thunderstorm rolled in. The sky went black, and the rain poured down. His resistance was over. Through his delirium, he heard the crash of thunder and saw a flash of lightning as he fell forward and the rope tightened.

But then he felt someone splashing water over his cracked and bleeding lips while someone else seemed to be rubbing his wrists. His legs had been propped up on a chair and he felt the blood pumping back into his body and arms. He could do nothing but cry out from the pain.

He soon became aware of who was working on him. It was the two investigators. They were crying out, "Don't die. We believe you now because we believe that your God performed a miracle by keeping you alive and then a flash of lightning cut the rope above your head just as you fell."

Pastor Chen was freed that day. And the two investigators and many of the prisoners were different in their faith from that day on.

We don't have to be like Pastor Chen to know that the Holy Spirit can bring transforming life into us. For every day, we encounter times in our lives when our faith is tested. It might be through a death of a loved one, it might be a serious illness, or any of the many curves or detours life hands us. But with the gift of the Holy Spirit that was brought forth on Pentecost over 2000 years ago, we are able to confront our doubts, our fears with a new endurance and willingness to go on, with the courage that only can be given through the Holy Spirit.

John tells us that "*This is the Spirit of truth, whom the world cannot receive, because it neither sees him nor knows him. You know him, because he abides with you and he will be in you.*"

He will be in us. That is our promise.

Mark 6:14–29
Better Than He Thought

The story of the beheading of John makes it crystal clear that God's work is risky. When you do it, don't expect accolades or success. When you speak the truth to the powerful there may be a bitter price to be paid. But, no matter what may happen, God's plan cannot be stopped.

Barbara Brown Taylor tells the story of a teacher who was fired from his job six months short of his retirement after 25 years. It was a nasty piece of work on the part of his superiors. They wanted to punish him for challenging them and to make him an example for anyone else thinking about trying the same thing. They called it early retirement and gave him a party he suffered through.

"I've been to my own funeral," he said weeks later, recounting the pain of it. "I lost my students, my program, my livelihood, and my pride. But you know what? There really is life after death. I'm doing things I always wanted to do, but never had time. I'm spending time with my wife. I'm finding energy I thought I'd lost forever. Getting crucified turned out better than I thought."

Mark 8:27-38

The Taizé Community

Jesus says to us in the above Gospel: *"Deny yourselves and take up your cross daily and follow me."*
One of the highlights of my sabbatical was the trip that Phil surprised me with . . . a trip to France. One of the significant spiritual experiences was when we took off in our rental car and drove across France to Taizé.

I was so excited! For years, I have begun nearly every morning listening to Taizé chanting as part of my morning meditation. I had always wondered exactly where all this incredibly beautiful and holy music came from.

So in our rental car from the de Gaulle airport, we maneuvered our way around Paris and drove across France. We were lost several times but finally made it to Macon, France, a city near Taizé.

The Taizé Community was founded by Roger Louis Schultz-Marsauche, later known simply as Brother Roger, born in 1915 in the village of Provence, Switzerland.

Roger was the son of a Swiss Reformed pastor. Brother Roger recalled that when he was twelve he saw his father go into a Roman Catholic church to pray, which was quite unusual.

About a year later, when Roger left home to attend secondary school, his parents sent him to lodge in the home of a poor Catholic widow, who had several children. Although lodging with another Protestant family was possible, his father thought the extra money would help the Catholic family more, despite the fact that this family came from a different tradition.

Being with this Catholic family influenced Roger significantly. In the summer of 1940, with only a short thesis to write to complete his theological degree, Roger decided to take a break from his education. Realize, at that time, several surrounding countries had already been overrun by Nazi Germany, and Roger felt that his academic pursuits were too far removed from the war that persisted around him.

He prayed and discerned what it really meant to live a life according to the Scriptures – to carry the cross of Jesus.

A year after this decision Roger reflected: 'The defeat of France awoke powerful sympathy. If a house could be found there, of the kind I had dreamed of, it would offer a possible way of assisting some of those most discouraged, those deprived of a livelihood; and it could become a place of silence and work."

Because his Swiss homeland was neutral and thus less affected by the war, he felt as if France would be ideal for his vision. For Roger, France was a land of poverty, a land of wartime suffering, yet a land of inner freedom. That is how he eventually settled in Taizé , a small desolate village just north of Cluny which is the birthplace of western monasticism.

In September 1940, Roger purchased a small house that would eventually become the home of the Taizé community. Only a few miles south of the separation line that divided a war-torn country in half, Roger's home became a sanctuary to countless war refugees seeking shelter.

Then on November 11, 1942, the Gestapo occupied Roger's house while he was in Switzerland collecting funds to aid in his ministry. Roger was not able to return to his home in Taizé until 1944, when France was liberated.

On Easter Day 1949, seven brothers committed themselves to a life following Christ in simplicity, celibacy and community.

Phil and I thought we were going to a simple monastic community so we were shocked when we came upon a community of several thousand young people from 17 to 25- years-of-age. They were from all over the world and they stayed with the Taizé community for usually one week. Each week a new group would arrive

As we heard bells ringing for prayers, we walked with the students to the church area where everyone sits on the floor and we awaited the brothers. In just a few minutes, the Taize monks entered and the chanting of scriptures began. It was if we were in heaven with young people singing as angels.

We found out that this community, though Western European in origin, seeks to welcome people and traditions from across the globe. This is reflected in the music and prayers where songs are sung in many languages, The music emphasizes simple phrases, usually lines from Psalms or other pieces of scriptures, repeated and sometimes also sung in canon. The repetition is intended to aid meditation and prayer.

Interestingly, these young people are orderly, respectful of each other and not going crazy in the food lines or basically any other time. They have no arts and crafts, no planned sporting activities, no strict rules. They live in tents and do not complain about the weather, the food or the conditions. They live in gratitude to God and love for others.

Yet, they willingly go to the Bible studies offered by the Brothers, they willingly study in small groups and they lovingly learn how to chant the scriptures.

The Taizé Community emphasizes that they do not want to create a movement or organization centered on the community. Rather they want to send these young people back from the youth meetings to their local churches, to their parishes, to their homelands, to undertake, with many others, a 'Pilgrimage of Trust on Earth.'

Phil and I found lodging for several nights in nearby Macon, but returned to Taizé in the morning.

We should all learn from this effort that was begun by Brother Roger many years ago. Sadly to say, the life of Brother Roger ended in 2005 by a fatal stabbing during an evening prayer service.

Brother Roger knew that to be a Christian is to be dominated by gratitude, obsessed by grace. Jesus said that if we wanted to follow Him, we must take up our cross daily. And this does not mean to simply endure whatever is thrust upon us by what some people call fate or bad luck.

A cross is an unforced, voluntary obligation. It means to offer some costly witness or ministry because our gratitude compels us. It is to be so grateful for all you have.

Dominated by gratitude, obsessed by grace. What a wonderful way of being.

2 Kings 5:1-15

That's Enough For Now

The above scripture reading, and those that the lectionary sets forth for the previous and following week, are all about healing. This reminded me of a venture that I was involved in several times a year for almost ten years. It was called the Journey of Healing. I was part of a volunteer team comprised of a priest, psychologist, a psychiatrist, nurse, nutritionist, exercise therapist and others. We were a multi-disciplinary team that understood God's healing touch and shared that knowledge with others.

And we were all on this journey, no matter how sick or scarred we were. It began when I was working on the Psycho-oncology team at the University of Miami Hospital. The first Journeys of Healing were for people diagnosed with cancer, and for their friends and families. We held it in the Florida Keys so we could have the healing environment of water, sunsets and fresh air. We held a Journey of Healing weekend two or three times a year.

After about a year, a friend of mine pointed out that those in pain and suffering from other illnesses, and from divorce, and death and other loss were in need of healing also. So, of course, we began offering it to all who felt the need for healing. We used the power of humor, we used the power of relationships, and of course we used the power of the scriptures. One of the scriptures we regularly reflected on was this Old Testament lesson, the story of Naaman.

The person that presented this reflection at the Journey of Healing was a person living with cancer. Her name was

Ellie. I wish I could tell you her exact words about Naaman. I will try.

Ellie would tell how she used to be like Naaman, using her intellect and monies to succeed. Naaman was a commander of the king's army, a "great man" before the king and highly decorated. Ellie had a high-status job, spoke several languages, and had earned her Ph.D.

Ellie did not have leprosy but had cancer for many years – and knew that not all people understood that disease, just as people in the Old and New Testaments did not understand leprosy.

Ellie would tell you that it took a lot for her to understand how powerful God is in her life. How healing sometimes is not physical but how the healing of a broken relationship was restorative to her. Ellie wrote an article after her first Journey of Healing weekend. She titled it: "It won't change your life - just the way you live it!" Here is part of what she wrote:

" 'It won't change your life, just the way you live it.' That's the slogan for The Florida Lottery and they may be on to something with their slogan - perhaps more than they realize. For, on a more personal and spiritual level, it also expressed the significance and possibilities of the Journey of Healing weekend.

"This weekend didn't change my life, just the way I live it. I am now able to move to that still center of my being which rests in God and in which God dwells. I am reassured that while my cancer may or may not be "cured" permanently, healing is taking place in my life as I seek a closer relationship with Christ. I am reminded through the Eucharist that resurrection is a daily experience in which our Lord comes to us offering new life, new hope, new joy, and a new chance to truly see others and minister to them. I know that I am not alone on this journey, this pilgrimage. I know many have their own 'cancers'. Others are walking the same path, and together we are able to comfort, encourage, and experience each other in an unique way as we share our stories of God's presence in our lives."

Ellie concluded, "With my luck, I'll probably never win the lottery, but with the grace and love of God, I'm being empowered to live with more abandon, more joy, more trust. And that's enough for now."

No, Ellie never did win the lottery, but she did live with more abandon, more joy, and more trust, right up until the time she left us to be with her Lord.

With Jesus, we are strengthened, we are never left alone, we are loved. That is our promise.

Fools for Christ

One evening shortly before Pentecost, at our Bible study, Gordon Scott said that he feels he needs to be a "fool for Christ" to help others understand his zeal and love.

What would you think of any of your fellow parishioners if you saw them on Main Street handing out tracts and inviting people to church? Would you join them or pretend you don't know them?

Gordon is not the only one that feels that way. Many people of the early church felt like "fools for Christ" because they knew that they had something to tell others.

Former Archbishop of Canterbury George Carey says, "Pentecost means that the church is challenged as a true sign of a community of Jesus Christ to the world. We must not be embarrassed if the values we stand for are in sharp contradiction to the world around us. If the character of the Spirit is indeed 'holy', then the sacramental nature of the Church demands that we are called to be holy, set apart, to be markedly different. That was the character of the early Church. It is meant to be our character today also."

It is wonderful to see you all wearing your red but don't just wear red today! Be bold about your fire for our Lord! It is Pentecost. Let this be the spark that puts you on fire for Christ. Let the Holy Spirit get hold of you. Don't let your light just shine; let it be a huge fire that cannot be extinguished. And as your fellow parishioner Gordon exclaimed, "Let's be fools for Christ".

Mark 10:35-45

The Empty Sack

What a blessing that we can drink our cup of life: slowly, tasting every mouthful - all the way to the bottom! Living the complete life is drinking our cup until it is empty, trusting that God will refill it with everlasting life. We are so very blessed to have the cup of Jesus. What we do about it is up to us. Not everyone understands the significance of blessings.

It is like the old legend of the three men and their sacks. Each man had to go through life with two sacks: one in front and the other tied on his back.

The first man carried all the bad things people had done to him in the front sack so he could be reminded of them. He never wanted to forget them. All the good things he had in life were in the back, hidden from view. He never saw the good things. Not one thought went to the positive things in his life, only the negative.

The second man carried all the good things in the front so he could show them off and all the bad negative things in life in the back. But every time he bragged and showed off his good things of life, they became a negative and they needed to go with all the other negative things in the back. The sack in the back became so heavy he could hardly move through life.

The third man carried positive thoughts, the blessings of his life and the thoughts of all the great things people have done for him, all in the front sack. That is where he could readily get to them and know how blessed he was. He said the sack was like 'a sail on a ship' and kept him going forward.

When asked about the sack on his back, he replied, "The sack on my back is empty. There's nothing in it because I have cut a hole in the bottom. In it I put all the negative things in life - either about myself or others. They go in one end and out the other, so I'm never carrying any extra weight at all. I don't even think of them."

When you are holding and lifting and drinking of the cup of Jesus, feel blessed. Know that Jesus is right there with you. *"The cup that I drink, you will drink."*

Know that you do not have to carry any extra weight of life for Jesus will let those negative things drop through the hole in your sack. None of us can go through this journey alone. God is with us. This is our promise.

God is Love

If you study the saints of the early church, you will know that they say that the Trinity is the most vital element of a spiritual life. This can be mystifying in itself. Yet if we look at the Trinity as "God is love' we see how true is the statement that the "Trinity is the most essential element to our spiritual life."

The following story illustrates this:

The father of a family possessed a miraculous ring. It had been passed down through generation after generation in the family to the son/heir. Whoever would wear this ring was endowed with special grace that made him extraordinarily kind, lovable, caring, and virtuous in every way. Never did he suffer a temptation to hurt anyone. Never did he even think a bad thought about anyone.

Up until this time there had been no problem in passing on the ring, because each generation had produced only one son as heir. This father, however, had three sons. The powers of the ring alerted him to the danger that the children who did not receive the ring would be jealous and not turn out well. To solve this problem the father had a jeweler fashion two rings identical to the magnificent original ring, and thus he left one ring to each of his three sons.

Upon receiving their inheritance, the first question each son asked was, "Which of us has the true ring?" They brought the rings to a renowned jeweler. He could not tell them apart, so perfectly did they match. Next they went to a wise old rabbi to seek his help.

The rabbi carefully studied the rings, and then asked the heirs: "Is not the purpose of the miraculous ring to make its wearer loving and kind, truthful and virtuous, caring and industrious?"

"Yes, Rabbi, that's the purpose," they replied in union.

"Then," said the rabbi, "it makes no difference which is the true ring. If each of you behave lovingly and kindly, truthfully and virtuously, caringly and industriously, each ring will become miraculous.

The father of those three sons taught them well. For he taught them about being in relationship with one another. They each accepted that their ring was just like the others. They knew how much their Father loved them.

Divine love is so tremendous – it is always in relationship. It does not happen alone. In the Trinity, the Father loves and so he begets the Son; the Son loves and so he gives his life for all mankind by dying for us on the cross; the love the Father and the Son have for one another is so great it causes a third Person to proceed from such love, and the Person is the Holy Spirit.

Be in that relationship and know that the love of God is the most necessary element in our spiritual life and God is love. The Father, The Son and the Holy Spirit in relationship is love. God has given his Son for us and through that the Holy Spirit dwells within us. We will never be alone.

John 14: 23–29

The Peace of God

One day an artist was commissioned by a wealthy man to paint something that would depict peace. After a great deal of thought, the artist painted a beautiful country scene. There were green fields with cows standing in them, birds were flying in the blue sky and a lovely little village lay in a distant valley. The artist gave the picture to the man, but there was a look of disappointment on the patron's face. The man said to the artist, "This is not a picture of true peace. It isn't right. Go back and try again."

The artist went back to his studio, thought for several hours about peace, then went to his canvas and began to paint. When he was finished, there on the canvas was a beautiful picture of a mother, holding a sleeping baby in her arms, smiling lovingly at the child. He thought surely, this is true peace, and hurried to give the picture to the wealthy man. But again, the man refused the painting and asked the painter to still keep trying.

The artist returned again to his studio. He was discouraged, he was tired and he was disappointed. Anger swelled inside him, he felt the rejection of this wealthy man. Again, he thought; he even prayed for inspiration to paint a picture of true peace.

Then, all of a sudden, an idea came and he rushed to the canvas and began to paint as he had never painted before. When he finished, he hurried to the wealthy man. He gave the painting to the man. The man studied it carefully for several minutes. The artist held his breath.

Then the man said, "Now this is a picture of true peace." He accepted the painting and paid the artist.

What was this picture of true peace? The picture showed a stormy sea pounding against a cliff. The artist had captured the furry of the wind as it whipped black rain clouds, which were laced with streaks of lightening. The sea was roaring in turmoil, waves churning, the dark sky filled with the power of the furious thunderstorm. And in the center of the picture, under a cliff, the artist had painted a small bird, safe and dry in her nest snuggled safely in the rocks. The bird was at peace midst the storm that raged about her.

Be that little bird in the nest amidst the turmoil of the storm. Have the peace that only God can give you. It is yours.

"Peace I leave with you; My Peace I give to you."

We each have a choice – to accept the inner peace given only by God or not to accept it. We also hear in the gospel that *"whoever loves me will keep my word."*

Jesus reminds us that it is easy to say we love him but it is far more difficult to obey him by accepting his love, grace and peace. You can easily spoil it for yourselves as we again hear from the Gospel according to Charlie Brown:

One day Lucy and Linus had a turkey wishbone and were going to pull it to make a wish. Lucy explained that if Linus got the bigger half, his wish would come true.

Linus asked, "Do I have to say it out loud?"

"Of course you do," said Lucy. Lucy went ahead and made her wish first. "I wish for six new sweaters, a new bike, a pair of skates, a new dress, and $100."

When it came time for Linus to make his wish, he said, "I wish for a long life for all my friends, and I wish for world peace."

At that, Lucy took the wishbone and threw it away, before they even broke it. "Linus, that's the trouble with you. You're always spoiling everything."

Don't spoil this love offering of God's. Don't throw the wishbone away before the wish is even granted.

It may seem difficult at times, maybe some times impossible, but our feeble efforts will be strengthened by the love of the Father - that same divine Father whose love is revealed in Jesus. And when we allow that divine love to flow through us, we enter into a mystical communion. Nothing could be more desirable.

Thanksgiving –
Not Just a Tradition

In an episode of the comic strip *Hi and Lois*, the family is gathered around the Thanksgiving table and one of the children asks, "Why do we always have turkey on Thanksgiving?"

Lois hesitantly answers, "Well . . . because it's a tradition."

The child asks, "What's a tradition?"

The other child interrupts to say, "A tradition is something we've been doing for so long we can't even remember why we do it."

Hopefully we have not forgotten what Thanksgiving is all about: We are to be thankful that we are thankful.

Trust

This gospel is the Parable of the Dishonest Manager. There are several truths Jesus is giving us, but this is story of a little girl named Jenny and her father is about trust:

Nine-year-old Jenny bought herself a five-dollar, dime store imitation pearl necklace. She loved those pearls. They made her feel dressed up and grown up. Jenny wore them everywhere - to church, to school and even to bed. She would not let her best friend or even her little sister wear her pearls.

Jenny had a very loving father and every night when she was ready to go to bed, he would stop whatever he was doing and come upstairs and read her a story. One night when he finished the story, he asked Jenny, "Do you love me?"

"Oh yes, Daddy. You know that I love you."

"Then give me your pearls."

"Oh Daddy, not my pearls. But you can have Princess - the white horse from my collection. The one with the pink tail. She's my favorite."

"That's okay, Honey. Daddy loves you. Good night." And he brushed her cheek with a kiss.

About a week later, after the story time, Jenny's father asked again, "Jenny, Do you love me?"

"Daddy, you know I love you."

"Then give me your pearls."

"Oh Daddy, not my pearls. But you can have my most favorite doll. She is so beautiful."

"That's okay, Jenny. Sleep well. God bless you. Daddy loves you."

And as always, he brushed her cheek with a gentle kiss.

A few nights later when her father came in, Jenny was sitting on her bed with her legs crossed Indian-style. As he came closer, he noticed her chin was trembling and then one silent tear rolled down her cheek.

"What is it, Jenny? What's the matter?"

Jenny didn't say anything but lifted her little hand up to her father. And when she opened it, there was her little pearl necklace. With a quiver, she finally said, "Here, Daddy, It's for you."

With tears gathering in his own eyes, Jenny father's reached out with one hand to take the dime-store necklace and with the other hand he reached into his pocket and pulled out a blue velvet case containing a small strand of genuine pearls and gave them to Jenny.

He had had them all the time. He was waiting for her to give up the dime-store stuff so he could give her the genuine treasure. She had to trust him with the thing she loved the most.

Jesus is telling us that if someone can be trusted with small things, they can be trusted with greater gifts. We are promised that if we can handle our resources well on earth, we will be entrusted with things more valuable than imaginable in heaven. That is the genuine treasure. The real genuine pearls.

The Light of the World

One summer when the youth group at our church came to spend a week with us at our home in North Carolina, we took them to visit Linville Caverns.

The caverns are not as large as perhaps Mammoth Cave in Kentucky, they are none-the-less impressive. As we approached the cave, the guide told us that the cave is quite large, and that the largest cavern is several hundred feet underground.

No light penetrates the hundreds of feet of rock and soil. The cavern at that depth is totally dark. A number of years ago electric lights had been installed throughout the cave. With the lights, thousands of visitors can now go into the furthest depths of the cave.

We slowly climbed down the stairs with curiosity and a bit of trepidation.

Once we reached the large cavern, hundreds of feet under the surface, the guide pointed out the lighting system. He said for us to be very still and then he turned off all the lights. The darkness was overwhelming.

We were not prepared for this. Your heartbeat accelerates; your blood pressure rises. Your eyes search in vain for any glimmer of light. There is nothing! You are sure that the guide will turn the lights on again but, for a few moments, you learn what it is like to be in complete darkness.

It was scary. We heard a few people gasp; several of us laughed out of nervousness and were trying to find a hand to hold. It seemed like forever even though just a few moments had passed. No light was evident. It made no difference whether your eyes were open or closed; it was all the same. You literally cannot see your hand before your face.

While the lights were still out, the guide asked how difficult did we think it would be to find our way out of the cave with the lights turned off.

You know that would be impossible, and any attempt would be only futile and also very dangerous, for without light you could not see the hazards, the slippery places, or tell the difference between a five-foot or a fifty-foot drop. The only way out would be to wait for someone to come in with a light.

And then the guide lit a match - just one match. That tiny light overwhelmed the darkness. Amazingly it lit up the whole cavern. Its light reached from wall-to-wall and from ceiling-to-floor. We each took a huge breath of relief and noticed that the other visitors to the cave were also expressing relief.

Everyone started smiling. Gradually our eyes became adjusted to the light. One little match made a huge difference.

Like the light of one child being born, that of Christ; and it makes a huge difference.

We hear about light in this scripture from John. In fact, light is mentioned twenty-three times in the Gospel of John.

"I am the light of the world," says Jesus. *"Whoever follows me will never walk in darkness but will have the light of life."* And we are the children of the light.

That day our children from church were shown the blessing of God's light in a different way.

Mark 13: 44-52

Like a Hidden Treasure

Why in the world did Jesus talk about the kingdom of heaven in metaphors? Why didn't he just come out and say it? If anyone is qualified to speak directly about God, surely it is Jesus. Yet he speaks about holy things compared to ordinary things . . . breaking into our everyday understanding of things and inviting us to explore them all over again.

The poet, Robert Frost, once wrote to his friend Sidney Cox, "Our minds are so crowded with what we have been told to look for that they have no room for accidental discoveries." Most of the things really worth finding in life are accidental discoveries.

Think about the way most people meet their future spouses. There was a young woman who turned around during the passing of the peace at her church and shook hands with a man sitting directly behind her. They were married 18 months later. I met my husband Phil on an escalator—I was going down the escalator and he was going up! Some of you met on the Internet.

The people who find the treasures are not the ones who grow tired of looking and lose interest; nor the ones who are already satisfied with life; nor those who are so discouraged that they give up.

We only have to be careful to keep our minds open to discoveries. If our minds are full of things we have been taught to look for, like a particular kind of religious experience, or a particular kind of religious community, or a particular kind of emotional or psychological or physical cure, we will not find the kingdom.

Words Beg to be Spoken

"But only speak the word, and let my servant be healed."

All Jesus needed to do was speak the words to heal the Centurion's slave. Words of healing.

To be sure, the healing ministry of Christ was unique but, as Christians, we have been given another grace; the witness of Christian fellowship with the ability to change another's condition, if only their attitude about their condition, by speaking a healing word.

The writer of Proverbs says it best: *"A word fitly spoken is like apples of gold in pictures of silver* (25:11)."

A man came out of his house on his way to church one Sunday morning. Across the yard, his neighbor was loading his golf clubs into a station wagon. The neighbor said, "Henry, do you want to play golf with me today?"

Henry, with an expression of self-righteous horror on his face, replied: "This is the Lord's Day and I always go to church. Sorry, I will not play golf with you today."

After a moment of embarrassed silence, the golfer said: "You know Henry, I have often wondered about your church and I have always admired your devotion. You know also, this is the seventh time I have invited you to play golf with me, and you have never even once invited me to go to church with you."

Sometimes, the words beg to be spoken.

Ephesians 2:8

None Would Score Even Close To A Hundred

St. Paul in his letter to the Ephesians tells us that there is no way we can earn God's favor. Christ has done that for us.

An Army chaplain was addressing the soldiers in his company one day. He said to them, "There are two possibilities following death. Heaven and hell. If you would like to know your destination I will be happy to give you a little test . . . the results of which will be your answer."

They answered in unison, "Okay. Give us the test."

They found some pencils and paper and the chaplain told them to number off ten spaces. Each question would count up to ten points. Each soldier was to grade himself on a scale from one to ten.

Question number one was, "Have you always loved God above all else and not put anything else before Him?"

Question two: "Have you ever misused God's name or made light of Him?"

There were other questions about family, God and conduct as the chaplain went through the Ten Commandments.

When the test was completed, he asked the men to tally up their scores. One soldier thought that he had scored quite well and had given himself a 75%, a passing grade in school.

One of the soldiers asked, "Say Padre, what's a passing score for this test, anyway?"

The chaplain answered, "100 points."

The men shook their heads. "You've got to be kidding! What's the use of trying? No one could be that perfect. Certainly we are all doomed."

The chaplain smiled and said, "I've got good news. There was a man who walked this earth and took this test and scored a 100 points. His name is Jesus.

"The purpose of the test is not to score a 100 points but to indicate our need for help. There is mercy and forgiveness for all who will receive it. Even though we may not score a 100 points, we can substitute his test score for our own. Because of what he has done, we are accepted. "

Eternal life is what grace is all about. The theme of God's unmerited and unrestrained love for sinners was so important to St. Paul that the word "grace" occurs 101 times in writings attributed to him. It only appears 28 times in all the rest of the New Testament.

When we understand that none of us would score even close to 100 but there is someone who has taken the test for us, we then will fill our hearts with humility and compassion for those who also will not pass the test.

Exodus 3:1–15

The Search Committee

There is a story about a very long, late evening with the search committee of a church. The search committee had been going over resume after resume with hopes of finding the right match for their church. They had found no one and the search had been going on for months. Tired of the whole process, they were going to call it a night when they came upon this letter of introduction from a candidate:

To the Search Committee: It is my understanding that you are in the process of searching for a new pastor, and I would like to apply.

I wish I could say I was a terrific preacher, but I can't preach - actually, I stutter a bit when I speak. I wish I could say that I have an impressive educational background but I can't - no college or seminary - just the school of hard knocks.

I wish I could say I bring a wealth of experience to the position, but I can't - I have never been a pastor before (unless you count the flock of sheep I have been shepherding.)

I wish I could say I have wonderful pastoral skills, but I can't - sometimes I lose my temper and have been known to get violent when upset. I once killed somebody, but I hope you will not hold that against me.

I wish I could say that I am young, but I can't -actually, I am almost 80 years old . . .but I still feel young.

You might be asking yourself, why in the world would I be applying to the position of the priest of your church?

Well, one afternoon recently, the voice of God spoke to me and said I had been chosen to lead. I admit I was a bit reluctant but . . .here I am. I look forward to hearing from you and leading you into an exciting new future.

Yours sincerely.

Signed, Moses.

Well, obviously the search committee here never received such a letter. And I thank God for that! I would never have been hired. Who could compete against Moses?

And That's What Heaven Is All About

There was a crowd of people standing at the exit of Wal-Mart waiting for a downpour of rain to die down so they could get to their cars in the parking lot. It was the kind of rain that gushes, like it is in a hurry to hit the earth. One person in that crowd was a little six-year-old girl, standing by her mother.

Suddenly the little girl loudly exclaimed, "Mom, let's run through the rain.

"No, honey," said the Mother. "We'll wait until it slows down a bit."

The little girl waited about another minute and repeated, "Come on Mom, let's run through the rain."

"We'll get soaked," replied the mother.

"No we won't, Mom. That's not what you said this morning," the girl said as she tugged at her Mother's arm.

"This morning? When did I say we could run through the rain and not get wet?"

"Don't you remember? When you were talking to daddy about his cancer, you said, 'God got us through this. He can get us through anything!'"

At that point, the entire crowd around them became silent. No one came or left. Everyone was still.

The mother paused for a moment and thought about what she would say. This was a moment of affirmation in this child's life. A time when innocent trust could be nurtured so that it will bloom into faith.

So the Mother said, "Honey you are absolutely right. Let's run through the rain. If God lets us get wet, maybe we just need a good washing." Then off they ran with the crowd watching and smiling and laughing.

This type moment is what Celtic Christians call a 'thin place' or a moment or place where the eternal seems to be just under the surface of the everyday. It is that moment when we can peek behind the veil of the everyday world and catch a fleeting glimpse of God. Moses experienced this at the burning bush and we can too. Let us be open to our 'thin places' during this Lent.

When we begin to glimpse those places, we come before the wonderful, patient mercy of God. No excuses, no hesitations. And that is what heaven is all about.

If One Member Suffers, All Suffer Together With It

There is a story of two men. One was born blind and the other crippled. To make up for each of their difficulties, they worked together. The blind man carried the crippled man on his back; the crippled man gave directions to lead the way. One had eyes and the other had feet – and it worked very well.

One day, they met a lion in the road. Hearing the lion roar and out of fear, the blind man threw off his friend and tried to run away.

The lion quickly killed the crippled man because he couldn't run away.

But the blind man was also killed because he couldn't see where to run.

Both men died because one forgot that their lives were bound up together. Only together could they be able to live their lives to the fullest. Only together could they learn to live out the meaning of their lives. Only together could they have lived.

Only together are we the body of Christ as we are the individual members of that body. Only together are we the community of Christ and we are all part of the community in our service and ministry of God.

This is Paul's message given in his Letter to the Corinthians: *If one member suffers, all suffer together with it; if one member is honored, all rejoice together with it. Now you are the body of Christ and individually members of it.*

Empty Your Cup

There was a university professor who went searching for the meaning of life. After several years and many miles, he came to the hut of a hermit, who was believed to be holy, and asked to be enlightened.

The holy man invited the visitor into his humble dwelling and began to serve him tea. He filled the pilgrim's cup and then kept on pouring so that tea was dripping onto the floor.

The professor watched the overflow until he could no longer restrain himself. "Stop! The cup is full. No more will go in."

"Like this cup," said the hermit, "you are full of your own opinions, preconceptions, and ideas. How can I teach you anything unless you first empty your cup?"

If we read with built-in biases and prejudices to this Gospel lesson, we will miss the power of its message. The lesson challenges us to open our eyes, our ears and our hearts; to empty ourselves and stop judging others on the basis of our norms, customs, and stereotypes.

Welcome Home Party

I don't know about you, but I just love this passage from Luke's Gospel. There are several themes on which one could preach, but the two main ones are about hospitality and forgiveness.

True hospitality is all about our love of God and our love for one another. No one is excluded from this love.

When you come into the grace of Christ, you are 'in love'. There is nothing better in this world than to be with the greatest love of your life. That love is with our Lord. Being here in this sanctuary, opening our hearts to God's love, kneeling at the altar and receiving God's love is the best thing that anyone can imagine.

Let that love be like the story of a young man who was in the army serving in a dangerous place. This young soldier had been away from home for a long time. He wrote to his mother and father saying, "I will be coming home soon. I don't know exactly when but when the powers in charge here think it's the right time, our company will be sent home."

His father wrote telling him how excited they were and that his mother was preparing to have all the relatives and friends around for a "Welcome Home" party.

The young man wrote back, "Mom and Dad, thank you for offering to give me a party, but there is just one thing that I want to ask of you. When I do get home, the first thing I want is one of those famous meals that only you can cook. I can smell it here already as I lay here on my bunk. And I want to sit at the table and just talk with you and Dad and just look at you and enjoy nothing else but the fact that we are there together. After all I've been through - and I have been involved in some really terrible and horrifying things – I just want to soak up that love that you have for me and share the love that I have for you. That's all I want."

Matthew 25:31–46

Missing Hands

In Germany after World War II, some American soldiers were cleaning up a large cathedral which had been hit by a bomb.

It was the task of one soldier to gather all the fragmented pieces of statues into a pile. He found a beautiful statue of Jesus that was completely intact except the hands were missing. He searched all through the rubble but could not find the missing hands. Finally he placed the handless statue on the altar and put a sign in front of it. The sign read as if Jesus were saying, "Your hands are my hands."

And how true that is. We are the Lord's hands in the world today by which He feeds the hungry. We are His eyes to see the oppressed. We are His mouth to proclaim the good news of salvation. We are His arms to lift up the downtrodden. We are the body of Christ in the world.

When we pray, "Lord won't you do something to feed the starving and help the elderly?"

He responds to us, "I already have. I created you.

Luke 9:18-24

Who Do /Say I Am?

And Jesus asks his disciples, *"But who do you say that I am?"* Was this like a mid-term exam question for the disciples?

"Who do *I* say I am?" is a question for each of us today.

Imagine a court scene and you are on the stand. Perhaps someone like Sam Waterson from *Law and Order* is questioning you. He is trying to determine if you are a Christian.

Would there be enough evidence of your belief to convince a jury beyond a reasonable doubt?

How would prove you were a Christian? Your church attendance, your baptismal certificate, your Bible with your name on it would not be enough to prove you were a Christian. These things are indications, but they wouldn't prove your devotion or conviction about who Jesus is in your life.

If you knew the Lord's Prayer or could recite the Nicene Creed that may begin to point your way to being a Christian. Your knowledge of the Bible would be evidence. Yet none of these things would be the same as a direct testimony.

Some other evidence that would point to you being a Christian would be if you pray and if you acted on the direction you receive from God. Whether you trust Jesus even when you don't want to trust is more evidence. That your actions reflect your beliefs in Christianity would be more evidence. How you treat the poor, the homeless, the destitute, and the marginal would also indicate to the jury that perhaps you were a Christian.

Your own identity is directly related to who your Lord is. Tell the jury who or what your Lord is and they'll know who you really are.

John 3:1-17

The Ultimate Gift

And Jesus says to Nicodemus, *"Very truly, I tell you, no one can enter the kingdom of God without being born of water and Spirit. What is born of the flesh is flesh, and what is born of the Spirit is spirit. Do not be astonished that I said to you, you must be born from above."*

The giver of life gives us the spirit of life . . . the ultimate gift.

Yet Nicodemus said to Jesus, *"How can these things be?"*

How can these things be? I've said that to myself many times.

When I worked as an RN at Jackson Memorial Hospital, I saw premature babies born weighing no more than the weight of the hymnal you were just holding. They could not breathe on their own and were hooked by tiny tubes to respirators.

Many people did not expect them to live . . . yet many of these children are now grown and have children of their own.

The spirit of life was breathed into them.

"Who Do *You* Say I Am?"
A Very Personal Story

I am an American and proud of it. I am married to Phil and proud of it. I am the mother of Philip and David and proud of it. I am a priest in the Episcopal Church and proud of it. But I have an identity that is more basic than all of these, for I am a sinner saved by Jesus Christ.

Ask me for some identification, I will show you my driver's license, my passport. I could give you my social security number, my marriage license, my tax form. Come into my office and you can see my diploma from Yale Divinity School and Berkeley Seminary. I will show you the ordination certificate that officially makes me a priest.

But if you really want to know who a person is, you'll have to look into their heart.

When you look into my heart you will see the cross of Jesus. You will see a child who does not remember when she did not love God. You will see a child whose parents did not bring her to Sunday school but for years a wise Sunday School teacher would pick her up every single Sunday to take her to church so that she could learn about the love of Jesus. You will see a child who wanted to be like Jesus in every way possible.

But when I was about 15-years-old that love of God was tested. It was back in the 1960's but I remember it as if it were yesterday. We had gone to Sunday school and it was time for the main service at 10 o'clock. There I was sitting quietly with my other teenage friends on the back row of the church. That was the best place to sit for we were able to write notes to each other without the elders of the church being aware of it.

As with every Sunday at that Baptist church in Miami, we began our service with a hymn. We all stood up to sing and just as we sang the first line of the first hymn, in walked three people a little late for the service. They walked up the aisle and took a seat in about the third row.

Now that in itself was not that unusual but that day it was, because this was a totally white congregation and the people who walked in were of darker skin.

Even though the singing continued, I could feel the tension mounting with stares, glares and haughty looks.

Personally, I did not think it was a big deal for we lived right next to a family from Jamaica, whom I loved like my own. For years, we shared meals with them, played with them. The Quallo's were more than friends, they were family. Leona Quallo was another mother to me and was always there to listen, to encourage and just be with me while my own mother was working.

And anyway, didn't this church where I grew up teach me how Jesus loved everyone? I remember the lyrics of the little Sunday School song, "Jesus loves the little children, all the children of the world, red, yellow, black and white, they are precious in his sight, Jesus loves the little children of the world."

Well, the opening hymn ended and we all sat down, except for a few elders of our church who came to the back of the church and began talking right behind where my friends and I were sitting. The readings were going on in the front of the church. Another hymn was announced and while we were singing our pastor came back to talk with the elders. After that hymn, the pastor of the church that I grew up in, the church that I loved, the church that taught me the love of Jesus asked the three people to leave!

I was stunned. I wanted to shout, "No, don't do that! Let them worship God with us!" I wanted to run, to hide, to cry. My shyness, my youth, or whatever kept me there, but as I walked out of that church on that Sunday morning, I said to myself that I will never go to that church again. I tried to talk to my Sunday school teacher about it on the silent ride home but she would not answer my questions.

The very next morning, in the Monday *Miami Herald*, there was an article about how there had been a sit-in for civil rights at many of the churches in Miami and that my church was the only church that asked the people to leave.

I decided right then that I would not go to any church ever again.

And Jesus asks, *"Who do you say I am?"*

Who is Jesus to me? I would answer that he is the most sustaining person in my life. Someone that would not let me stray too far away.

Many Sundays went by after that Sunday and I was miserable. I had not been back to church. After hearing my story, my girlfriend Myriam del Castillo asked me to come to her Roman Catholic Church. I was a little frightened for I had never before been inside a church with statues and crosses. But I loved my friend and I knew I still loved Jesus. Myriam and I were close because our fathers had died about the same time when we were in seventh grade together.

I continued to go to that Catholic Church until a few years after that when I met my husband Phil and our first date was to St. Stephens Episcopal Church in Coconut Grove.

And as Paul Harvey would say, "and now you know the rest of the story."

Jesus was to me the love he always was, he taught me that he would never abandon me, never leave me alone. Indeed, the church at that time was caught up in disorder - trying to sort things out. And things are much different now in that church in Miami. But for a shy young girl at the age of 15, I knew who Jesus was in my heart and I thank God for that every day.

I don't know if I would be able to convince a jury that this is who I am, but I sure hope I could. I know beyond understanding that today I would not be quiet for any injustice to others and I will shout at the top of my lungs if necessary that Jesus was and will always be the love of my life.

John 13:31-35

Thou Shall

In this Gospel we learn of the new Commandment. After Judas has left to betray him, Jesus says to the disciples, *"I give you a new commandment, that you love one another. Just as I have loved you, you also should love one another."*

This was the farewell commandment. Jesus wanted them to be prepared. He wanted them to know what he expected of them. Ironically, his first concern was not a doctrine or theological truth but relational. He wanted his disciples to be known by their love for one another.

This new commandment was positive and open-ended. Rather than focusing on, *"Thou shalt not"*, this is a *"Thou shall."* This is very broad, while the Old Testament commandments are very specific. There is always a need for more love, so there is no end to this requirement.

But there is something else to this commandment; it is not only to love one another, but also love one another as I have loved you.

In what many who read the Sunday comics call the *Gospel according to Charlie Brown*, Lucy stands with her arms folded and with a resolute expression on her face, while Charlie Brown pleads with her, "Lucy," he says, "You must be more loving. The world needs love. Make this world a better place, Lucy, by loving someone else."

At that Lucy whirls around angrily and Charlie goes flipping over backwards, "Look, you blockhead," Lucy screams. "The world I love. It's people I can't stand!"

Perhaps we can understand Lucy's perspective. It is easy to love in the abstract. We can love the world, but sometimes it is the people around us that drive us crazy. It is precisely those people that Jesus called us to love.

They may be some of the people with whom we work, or go to school with, or live next door.

If we as Christians, who have the love of Jesus to model, cannot love, how can we expect others to love? The truth is that we love because God first loved us.

There is no better rule of life than loving others as Jesus loved us.

Ice Fishing

On a cold winter morning, a couple of men in Wisconsin figured that they would go out and do some ice fishing. So they found a nice patch of ice and proceeded to chip a hole in it and lowered their lines. But about a minute later, they heard a booming voice say: "There are no fish there."

So the two men looked at each other and wondered whose voice that was. They weren't sure but they figured that maybe it would be best if they moved over a little bit. And so they went over about 10 yards or so, and chipped another hole in the ice and fished there.

But once more, they heard a booming voice say: "I tell you again, there are no fish there."

And so the two men looked at each other in astonishment, still not knowing whose voice they were hearing. So, one more time they moved over another 10 yards, chipped a third hole in the ice, and dropped their lines.

But once more the booming voice said: "I'm telling you one last time, there are no fish there."

Finally, and very timidly, one man looked up to the sky and said: "Is that you, God?"

And the voice answered: "No, this is the owner of this ice skating rink. I'm trying to let you know that there are no fish there."

Simon Peter, James and John said, *"We have worked all night long but we have caught nothing."* They had been out all night long. They were fishermen. They knew where the fish were suppose to be. Their livelihood depended on the fish they brought in each morning. Their fathers, who were taught by their grandfathers, had taught fishing to them. They did exactly what they should have done, but there were no fish there.

And then Jesus came along!

Something to Ponder

Nancy, a college freshman was called on to give a demonstration speech, one of the four basic types of speeches everyone had to offer during the term in Freshman English. She took her place at the lectern and stood there, wordless, for almost the whole time allotted for the speech - three to five minutes. There was much nervous shifting and fidgeting in the room. Most thought she had forgotten what she wanted to say and was paralyzed. Finally, to everyone's surprise, she uttered only three words: "Silence is golden," and returned to her seat. She received an A.

A Simple Gesture
Of Acceptance

This scripture is about faith in God: *For in it the righteousness of God is revealed through faith for faith; as it is written. The one who is righteous will live by faith."* We are told to have faith and trust and not to be afraid.

As a priest and as a nurse, I have been involved in some mission activities where one's faith is tested daily. This story is about how the faith of a missionary surgeon working in India was tested.

A doctor came upon a man named John who was a leprosy patient in an advanced stage of the disease. This happened many years ago, but leprosy is still prevalent in some areas of the world today. Leprosy is a terrible disease that somewhat equates to the end stages of AIDS. The person with leprosy is rejected by their community and is sent to live in a leprosarium, similar to the old TB sanatoriums.

Little could be done for John surgically since both his feet and hands had already been damaged irreparably. He was given a place to stay and employment in the New Life Center, a community set up to house all those who were recovering from illnesses. Because of one-sided paralysis, John could not smile normally. When he tried, the uneven distortion of his features would draw attention to his paralysis. People often responded with a gasp or a gesture of fear, so John learned not to smile.

When his eyelids had to be stitched partially closed to protect his sight, John grew more and more paranoid about what others thought of him. He caused terrible problems socially at the Center. He stole, treated others cruelly, resisted authority and would even organize hunger strikes against the ones caring for him.

But throughout all of this, the missionary doctor took a liking to John. He talked to him about how he was loved by Jesus. After a while, John asked to be baptized and was baptized in a cement tank on the grounds of the New Life Center. Even with this, John still remained bitter to those around him. The scars of rejection and mistreatment were deeper than the scars and disfigurement of the leprosy.

One day, surprisingly, John asked the doctor what would happen if he visited the local church in town. John had never been to church. The doctor thought this might be some sort of defiant test, but wanted John to be able to attend the services. He knew he would first have to go to the church leaders to explain John's deformities. That night the doctor was on his knees asking God to give him the faith to see this through.

The next day, he explained to the church ministers how John was and that John asked to go to their church on Sunday. The doctor also asked if John could take the communion, knowing it would be from the common cup. He assured them that the disease was not contagious. The church leaders said "Yes, it would be fine if he came and he was welcome to partake of communion."

OK, now it was all right with the leaders, but how would the church community receive John? The doctor began thinking about backing out of this undertaking, not wanting to see John hurt after all the progress he had made. But that night in prayer he felt God was asking him to have faith to get John through this.

With many misgivings, the doctor took John to the little church the next Sunday. They walked the distance to the church, a plain, whitewashed brick building with a corrugated tin roof. It was a very tense moment for both of them. John was physically trembling, which showed his inner turmoil. The doctor's prayer was: "Please God, let no church member show the slightest hint of rejection. Please Lord, give us both faith to endure this."

As they entered the church during the singing of the first hymn, an Indian man toward the back half-turned and saw them. And then it happened. The man put down his hymnal, smiled broadly, and patted the chair next to him, inviting John to join him. John was startled. Haltingly, John made shuffling half steps to the row and took his seat. The doctor breathed a prayer of thanks.

A simple gesture of acceptance may not seem like much, but it can be decisive. For John, after a lifetime of being judged on his own physical image, he had finally been welcomed on the basis of another image: The image of God.

Love One Another

I am reminded of a story about a minister who had preached on this very familiar gospel many times over the years but was not sure if the message was really reaching his people.

So beginning his next sermon on this scripture he stood up and said, "Love one another" and then sat down.

There was deafening silence in the church.

After a few minutes he stood up again and said, "Love one another" and again sat down.

The congregation began to whisper and become restless. After a few more minutes he stood up once more and said, "Love one another."

And again he sat back down. Now a general stirring moved through the people as he for one final time stood and said, "Love one another" and sat down.

The people in the church did not what to make of this and were somewhat dumbfounded when finally an older man in the congregation stood up and spoke, "I think I understand what Pastor means. He wants me to love you," as he pointed to someone in the pew behind him. "But how can I love you, when I do not know you?"

With that, he introduced himself and began to get to really know the people behind him. Others got up from their pews. Phone numbers were exchanged. Dinner invitations were extended. People were getting to really know and love one another.

It Will Teach Him a Lesson

In this Gospel, Jesus was teaching Simon and the Pharisees several lessons. One of them was about forgiveness.

That reminds me of the incident of an old rancher, tough and mean. One day, one of his cowboys was caught stealing. When he was dragged before the rancher and the old rancher looked down on him, the cowboy trembled in his boots.

"Hang him," said the rancher, "It will teach him a lesson."

Time came for the old rancher to die. He found himself before God. When God looked down at him, the old rancher thought about his life and all the mean things he had done. He trembled in his boots.

"Forgive him," said the Lord, "It will teach him a lesson."

Again Luke is writing to help us see how Jesus would see through his eyes -- not on the basis of outward appearances, but much deeper, from the heart. Only then will we discover the power of love, forgiveness, inclusiveness and acceptance.

John 2:1-11

Make Sure
You Invite Jesus

Years ago when Johnny Carson was the host of *The Tonight Show*, he interviewed an eight-year-old boy.

The boy was asked to appear because he had helped rescue two friends in a coal mine outside his hometown in West Virginia.

As Johnny questioned the boy, it became apparent to him and the audience that he was a Christian. So Johnny asked him if he attended Sunday school. When the boy said he did Johnny inquired, "What are you learning in Sunday school?"

"Last week," came his reply, "our lesson was about when Jesus went to a wedding and turned water into wine."

The audience roared, but Johnny tried to keep a straight face. Then he said, "And what did you learn from that story?"

The boy squirmed in his chair. It was apparent he hadn't thought about this. But then he lifted up his face and said, "If you're going to have a wedding, make sure you invite Jesus!"

The little boy was on to something.

Where Are Your Scars?

On an early morning in December several years ago, someone threw a rock through the window of a home in Newton, Pennsylvania. It was the third day of Hanukkah, and the home belonged to the Markovitz family, who are of the Jewish faith. The vandals reached into the broken window, grabbed the electric menorah inside, and smashed it to the ground.

The people in the neighborhood took this seriously, and they took it hard. They were pained that a hate crime could happen in their neighborhood, fearful that it foreshadowed greater violence.

One of the neighbors, Margie Alexander, decided to do something about it. She went from home to home visiting her neighbors and explained what they could do to help, to show support for the Markovitz family. Many neighbors would not even talk with her.

But Margie was persistent and within a few days, on the next-to-last day of Hanukkah, twenty-five Christian homes in the neighborhood displayed brightly burning menorahs in their windows.

The vandals never returned, and, as the lights burned on, barriers between people were broken and love overcame hate, at least for some.

One neighbor announced that the whole experience had changed her feelings toward those different from herself and said that she planned to put out a menorah again every Hanukkah.

If we have not been rejected for living our faith like Jesus was, we might look into how we have been living our faith.

In heaven we will look at Jesus, the scars still in his hands and feet; and he will look at us. And if we have no scars, no marks of helping others, he will simply say: "Was there nothing to fight for?"

Luke 5:1–11

Enjoy Life

There is a story about a rich industrialist who was disturbed to find a fisherman sitting lazily beside his boat. "Why aren't you out there fishing?" he asked.

"Because I've caught all the fish I need for today," said the fisherman.

"Why don't you catch more fish than you need?" the rich man asked.

"What would I do with them?" asked the fisherman.

"Sell them. You could make more money," came the impatient reply, "and then buy a better boat so you could go out further and catch more fish. You could purchase nylon nets, catch even more fish, and make more money. Soon you'd have a fleet of boats and be rich like me."

The fisherman asked, "And then what would I do?"

"Then you could sit down and enjoy life,"

"What do you think I'm doing now?" the fisherman replied.

Thank You, Thank You, Lord Jesus

Years ago, Dr. Theodore Stevenson was a visiting surgeon in a mission hospital in western India during Christmas. It was a hot, dirty, smelly place with many very ill persons. He states that this was his most memorable Christmas. Here is his Epiphany story:

The Christian staff of the mission hospital presented a pageant, complete with live animals and even a real baby borrowed from the nursery with permission of the mother. A crowd of townspeople watched with interest. After the usual cast of characters had gathered around the manger, and the choir sang, a young woman wearing a white sari and a nurse's cap stepped onto the stage and knelt before the manger. She spoke of her service to Christ.

Next was an Indian workman carrying a hoe, one of the maintenance staff. This man knelt before the manger, then announced to the startled audience that he had once had leprosy and had been doomed to a life of begging. He then told how the caring Christian medical staff had treated him and performed surgery on his once useless hands.

Then to the surprise of all, a beloved surgeon, Dr. Chopade, wearing operating room scrubs, came to the manger and bowed low before it. Then rising to his feet, the doctor stated that no one present knew that he had been born an "untouchable" himself.

He had been a member of the lowest social and religious caste of the Hindu culture! A murmur of disapproval rumbled with the people because "untouchables" were not supposed to become doctors and especially not surgeons.

He told them all about his wretched boyhood, in which he and his family were segregated from the rest of the village. The food for the family came from garbage heaps.

He told how he was prohibited from going to the village school or using the village well.

Some angry voices from the audience shouted that he had only experienced what he deserved. That he should not be a doctor.

Dr. Chopade quietly continued, telling about his eventual encounter with a kind mission doctor, who had inspired Chopade to become a doctor himself. It was a difficult journey but with the help of missionaries, he finally graduated from college and medical school.

He told them all in simple language that all he wanted to do in life was serve the Lord and that is why he came back to this village to be a surgeon.

Then this noted surgeon from the untouchables put his palms together in the traditional Indian greeting, he turned to the manger, bowed his head and said, "Thank you, thank you, Lord Jesus."

Every person in the audience, even those who demeaned him . . . they all stood and bowed saying "Thank you, thank you, Lord Jesus."

The wise men knelt, worshiped and adored. And then they offered the gifts, as did this surgeon.

Let us be as wise as the wise men. First, be open to the mysterious reality of God in our midst and the many ways that this holy presence is manifested. Second, seek out with deliberation, trusting that God's grace will lead you. Third, kneel before your Lord and offer your gifts and thank him.

Basic Fundamentals

The Ten Commandments are the basic fundamentals, the foundation of values for our behavior.

Biblical scholars surmise that the Ten Commandments were put in their present form during the period of Exile (587-538 B.C.). The commandments have been divided into two sections. The first through the fourth commandments are concerned with religious duties: The second section is about our relationship with others.

Some of the commandments seem easier to keep than others. Most people do not even know all of them. In fact, a Gallop poll stated that even though 80% of Americans believe that the Ten Commandments are still valid for today, less than half of that 80% can name even five of them.

Keeping the Sabbath is a basic one. Sandy Koufax, one of the greatest baseball pitchers of all time, had a left arm like the sling of David.

His team, the Los Angeles Dodgers, was in the 1965 World Series and Koufax was scheduled to pitch the opening game. But Koufax, who was Jewish, announced that he would not play that day as it was Yom Kippur, the holiest day of the year.

"But it is the World Series," the team owners and managers pleaded, "Can't you at least pitch a few innings?"

Koufax was firm in his refusal and his commitment to his faith. Later in the series, however, Koufax pitched shutouts in games five and seven, and the Dodgers won the series, four games to three.

What commitment to God do you not waver?

Please, Don't Go So Fast

Vince Lombardi, legendary football coach of the Green Bay Packers knew his work was cut out for him when he first went to Green Bay.

The Packers had lost over and over again, season after season. They thought of themselves as losers, not winners.

After a disastrous exhibition of football in a pre-season game, Coach Lombardi gathered the team together in the locker room. "Men, we will be going back to the basic fundamentals of the game."

Seeing that he had their attention, Coach Lombardi continued, "In case you have forgotten, this is a football."

Max McGee, one of the most talented players on the team, said, "Coach, please don't go so fast."

Let us also go back to the basics: In this scripture, in case we have forgotten, are the Ten Commandments.

A Baptism Story

An Episcopal priest in Ohio tells this story:

A 10-year-old boy from his congregation, named Cameron, walked into his office one afternoon and said he needed to talk to him.

Cameron was fresh from soccer practice; he was wearing his Cincinnati Reds baseball cap. But it wasn't sports Cameron wanted to talk about; he had a request for his pastor.

"I'd like to be baptized," Cameron said. "We were learning about Jesus' baptism in Sunday School last week and the teacher asked the class who was baptized. All of the other kids raised their hands, but I didn't. I want to be baptized too."

Using his best pastoral tone of voice, the priest said, "Cameron, is the reason you want to be baptized just so you can be like everyone else?"

His freckles winked up at him and he replied, "No. I want to be baptized because it means I belong to God."

His pastor was touched by his understanding.

"Well, then," he said, "How about we baptize you next Sunday?"

Cameron's smile turned to concern and he asked, "Do I have to be baptized in front of all those people in the church? Can't I just have a friend baptize me in the river?"

The priest asked from where had he come up with that idea.

"Well," the boy said, "Jesus was baptized by his cousin John in a river, wasn't he?"

Caught off guard, the priest conceded, "You have a point. But," he asked, "if a friend baptized you in the river, how would the church recognize it?"

Realizing this was a teachable moment, he reached for his Book of Common Prayer; but before he had even placed his hand on the book, Cameron responded with these unforgettable words: "They will know by my new way of life."

"They will know me by my new way of life."

Aren't Sunday School teachers wonderful!

The Heavenly City
Of His Dreams

Then he said, "Jesus, remember me when you come into your kingdom."

This old Jewish folktale speaks of the kingdom that God offers us; not the kingdom of power and success and individual achievement, but a kingdom of the kind of love and connection and compassion that Jesus lived and died for:

There was a once a poor man who grew tired of the corruption and hatred that he saw every day. He was tired of the constant injustice that his people experienced, and the loneliness of his isolated living.

His family and friends listened as he spoke with passion of his desire for a city where justice was honored and where personal wholeness could be found.

Night after night he dreamed of a city where heaven touched earth.

One day he announced that he could wait no longer. He packed a meager meal, kissed his wife and children goodbye, and set out in search of the magical city of his dreams.

He walked all day and just before the sunset, he found a place to sleep at the edge of the road, near a forest. He ate his meal, said his prayers and smoothed the earth where he would sleep.

Just before he went to sleep, as was the practice, he placed his shoes in the center of the path, pointing in the direction he would continue the next day.

That night a sly fellow was walking the same path and discovered the traveler's shoes. Unable to resist a practical joke, he turned the shoes around, pointing them in the direction from which the man had come.

Early the next morning the traveler arose, said his prayers, ate some food and continued his journey by walking in the direction his shoes pointed.

He walked all day long, and just before sunset he saw the heavenly city off in the distance. It wasn't as large as he had expected, and it looked strangely familiar.

He entered a street that looked much like his own, knocked on a familiar door, greeted his family and lived happily ever after in the heavenly city of his dreams.

Brothers and sisters, the kingdom of God where Christ reigns as our King is not somewhere else; it is here, where we live. It is here in our hearts. It is here in our souls. It is found in our brokenness, in our shattered lives, in our pain, in our sadness, wherever our hunger is the deepest. It is found in the joy of reconciliation, in our triumphs and in our happiness.

Lost in the Wilderness

When Leonardo da Vinci was painting his masterpiece "The Last Supper" he looked unceasingly for a model for his Christ. At last, he located a chorister in one of the churches in Rome who was lovely in life and features, a young man named Pietro Bandinelli.

DaVinci worked off-and-on on the painting. Years passed, and the painting was still unfinished. All the disciples had been painted save one - Judas Iscariot.

Now da Vinci started to look for a model for Judas; he looked for a man whose face was hardened and distorted by sin.

At last he found a beggar on the streets of Rome with a face so villainous that da Vinci shuddered when he looked at him. He hired the man to sit for him as he painted the face of Judas on his canvas.

When he was finished and about to dismiss the man, da Vinci said: "I have not yet found out your name."

"I am Pietro Bandinelli. I also sat for you as your model of Christ."

What happened to Pietro Bandinelli in those years while da Vinci was painting "The Last Supper?"

We don't know, but this reminds me of a billboard that catches my eye every time I drive on I-40 to Asheville.

This billboard shows an attractive woman and then a picture of another woman who I assumed was a different person at least 15 years older. The headline on the billboard read: "three years later." Underneath the two very different pictures is the caption: "What meth does with one's life."

What happens to some people can be because of the temptation of sin. It is something we all face. The very thing that Jesus faced with the devil in the wilderness.

The wilderness can be a place where spiritual lessons are learned and spiritual discipline is practiced. When we find ourselves in our own wilderness, often our tendency is to flee as fast as possible and usually that doesn't work.

A reflective, spiritual response would be, "God why have you led me to this wilderness? What am I to learn from it? Stay with me, lead me and show me your path through the wilderness, dear Lord."

Basement or Balcony?

In Joyce Landorf's book, *Balcony People*, people are described as falling into two categories: basement people and balcony people.

Basement people only criticize and point out the negative. They tell us what we are not - not what we can be.

Landorf describes the balcony: "All around that sphere of clear air in our conscious minds runs a balcony filled with people who are not merely sitting here, but are practically hanging over the railing, cheering us on." It is like having a cloud of witnesses both past and present smiling down and saying, "Go, Go, you can do it."

Habitat for Humanity

The 1970's and 1980's have now been labeled as the "Me Generation" and the "Greed Generation." It seemed that a man named Millard Fuller fit right into these categories. He was a modern-day version of the rich, young ruler and Zaccheus rolled into one. Millard began making money in great abundance and by the time he was 30-years-old, he was a self-made millionaire. But his marriage was in trouble because of all the time and attention he gave to his work.

One day his wife took their two children and left him. His life began to crumble. He decided right then to change his goal of being an ambitious, self-centered, driven millionaire and become a man of faith and mission for God.

In an attempt for reconciliation, he and his wife went to a mission project at a place in Georgia named the Koinonia Farms to spend time rebuilding their marriage.

While he was at the Koinonia Farms, he had a clear vision of what he needed to do. It was to build suitable, affordable housing to replace shanties and shacks of people in the rural areas trapped in the vicious cycle of poverty and despair.

That program today is Habitat for Humanity. Millard gave away his millions and took up a mission of compassion.

Millard Fuller said, "I don't believe that we are saved by how many houses we put up. I don't believe we are saved by how many poor people we feed. I believe that we are saved by the blood of Jesus and the grace of God.

"But what is our response to Jesus' sacrifice and the grace of God? For me and others, Habitat for Humanity is the response of what has been done in Christ for us."

Cheer Them On To Health

The first time my sons came to St. Francis Episcopal Church, Rutherfordton, NC was at my very first service. It was Christmas Eve, 2003.

Afterward, we talked about how wonderful the service was that evening.

It is a tradition at St. Francis that when reaching that part of the Prayers of the People, when the names for whom special prayer requests have been made, instead of the Intercessor reading aloud the names, as is usually done, the congregation in unison says out loud the first names of the people.

My son Philip commented how saying each name in unison was as if we were cheering them on into health. "Go Jesse, Go Wanda, Go Michael!"

That is a good thought to remember as we pray for those who are in need.

Exodus 3:1–15

Jehovah is Still God!

Above all else, we are to trust God. This story is from the book *The Hidden Price of Greatness*:

Gladys Aywlard, missionary to China almost eighty years ago, was forced to flee when the Japanese invaded Yangcheng. But she could not leave her work behind. With only one assistant, she led more than a hundred orphans over the mountains toward Free China.

During Gladys's harrowing journey out of war-torn Yangcheng . . . she grappled with despair as never before. After passing a sleepless night, she faced the morning with no hope of reaching safety.

A 13-year-old girl in the group reminded her of their much-loved story of Moses and the Israelites crossing the Red Sea.

"But I am not Moses," Gladys cried in desperation.

"Of course you aren't," the girl said, "But Jehovah is still God!"

When Gladys and the orphans made it through, they proved once again that no matter how inadequate one feels, God is still God and we can trust in him. May we, as grateful children, welcome his Spirit as God sets our hearts ablaze!

Jehovah will always be God. And with God, all things are possible.

Gladys' story was made into a wonderful film, *The Inn of the Sixth Happiness*, starring Ingrid Bergman.

Only Passing Through

There was a young girl named Clara who lived on a street right next to a cemetery. Her school was straight across, on the other side of the cemetery. Not unlike many children, the neighborhood children were all frightened of the cemetery. In fact, they took great pains to avoid it, walking all the way around it to get to the school, and then all the way around it again to come home.

But not so with this girl. Every morning Clara would walk straight through the cemetery to school. And at the end of the day she would walk back, straight through, to come home, usually singing along the way.

An elderly neighbor sat on her porch each day and watched and wondered. One afternoon, she called Clara over as she returned from school and said to her, "My young friend, I notice that every day, all the children on our block walk around the cemetery to go to school and back, but you just walk right through. How can you do that? Doesn't it frighten you to walk so close to death?"

And the young girl replied, "No. I'm not frightened, because I know that I'm only passing through."

This story reminds me of this collect that bids us to pray for an abundance of God's mercy, that with God as our ruler and guide, *"we may so pass through things temporal, that we lose not the things eternal."* Living faithfully has everything to do with how we pass through our daily lives. Living faithfully means always being connected with God as our ruler and guide, as with one another.

The way we pass through life each day – the way we walk – does matter.

Daddy, Is Your Face Toward Me?

There is a story of a young man whose wife had died, leaving him with a five-year-old son. Back home from the cemetery on the day of the funeral, they went to bed early because in his sorrow the young widower could think of nothing else he could bear to do. As he lay there in the darkness, grief stricken, numb with sorrow, the little boy broke the stillness from his little bed with a disturbing question: "Daddy, where is Mommy?"

The young father tried to answer his son and tried to get him to go back to sleep, but the question kept coming from his confused, tired young mind: "Where is my Mommy? When is she coming home?"

After a while, the father got up and brought his son to bed with him. But the child was still disturbed and restless . . . persistent with his probing, heartbreaking questions.

Finally the little boy reached out his hand through the darkness searching for his father's face, asking, "Daddy is your face towards me?"

Given assurance, both verbally and by his own touch that his father's face was indeed toward him, the little boy said, "If you face is toward me, I think I can go to sleep." And in a little while, he was quiet and asleep.

The father lay there in the darkness and in child-like faith prayed: "O God, the way is dark and I confess that I do not see my way through right now, but if your face is toward me, somehow I think I can make it."

You and I can make it through the darkness of times. You see, God's face is always toward us . . . watching us, gently guiding us. So weeping may spend the night but joy comes in the morning.

Matthew 4:12–23
The Greatest Sentence

This is a short story about a school teacher who had her fifth grade students pick a sentence, which they believed was the greatest sentence ever written. They were to write the sentence, name the author and tell why the sentence was important.

Most of the children selected wonderful sentences of Abraham Lincoln, or Martin Luther King, Jr, or from the United States Constitution.

One girl's sentence was not written by anyone famous. It was written by the girl's new stepfather. It was written in ballpoint ink on the back of a picture postcard from Hawaii, where her new stepfather and her mother were on their honeymoon.

"What is it that makes this sentence important?" the teacher asked the fifth grader.

The girl explained: "Until I received this postcard, I never know how my stepfather felt about me."

The sentence on the back of that postcard read simply: "Charlotte, I love you."

Know that the greatest sentence written is written for you. God loves you.

Wonderful Are Your Works

Most children begin their dinner prayer with "God is Great, God is Good." Psalm 139, one of my favorites, is attributed to David and talks clearly of the greatness of God. In the Psalms we are told more about God than we are told practically anywhere else in the Bible, and this psalm describes for us just how awesome God really is.

To understand how truly great God is, one needs to read the children's book by Robert Wells titled: *Is A Blue Whale The Biggest Thing There Is?*

The largest animal on earth is the blue whale. Just its tail fin is bigger than most animals on earth. But a blue whale isn't anywhere near as big as a mountain. If you could put one hundred blue whales inside of a huge jar, you could put a million of those whale jars inside a hallowed-out Mount Everest.

If you stack one hundred Mount Everests on top of one another, it would be just a whisker on the face of the earth.

One million earths can fit inside our sun.

Fifty million of our suns can fit inside of super star Antares. Antares and billions of other stars make up the Milky Way Galaxy.

But the Milky Way Galaxy isn't anywhere near as big as the universe. There are billions of other galaxies in the universe.

The One who created it all spoke it into being and sustains it with His love.

How awesome God really is. That He, though being omnipotent, omniscient, and omnipresent, can live in our hearts through faith in Jesus Christ.

More wondrous than the stars that twinkle, the sun that shines, the moon that glows, the lightning that strikes, the thunder that roars, the snow that falls, or the ice that freezes, is what you can see in the mirror.

Can we truly feel the same way as David when he wrote: *"I praise you, for I am fearfully wonderfully made. Wonderful are your works; that I know very well."*

We Are the Lost Sheep;
We Are the Lost Coin

In this Gospel Jesus tells us about being lost.

This reminds me of a time when our sons Philip and David and the grandchildren were here visiting. We were all super hungry and Phil was in the kitchen whipping us up something for dinner. Dinnertime was still nearly an hour away so we walked to the beach to watch the sunset. We became aware of a man in his 60's yelling at the top of his lungs: "Sam! Sam! Sam!"

A few people and I approached the man and found out that his five-year-old grandson was nowhere to be found. "He was right here a minute ago."

This was a grandfather who was entrusted by his son to take care of the child when they came to the beach. His wife had already started walking the beach in search of Sam. We found out what he looked like: skinny, brown hair, "this tall", wearing red shorts. He did not have his shirt on and actually that was a concern because the air was getting a bit cool.

I stayed with the great-grandmother as my sons went to the Beach Café thinking Sam might have seen the swings and started to play. As I sat with this extremely anxious women we started to pray for Sam's safe return.

The grandfather began knocking on the doors of the homes on the beach. No Sam.

The police had been called and they were searching also. Over an hour went by, sunset had happened and night was approaching . . . still no Sam. We prayed and prayed and prayed.

Then suddenly, we heard on a policeman's phone that Sam had been found way up the beach, past the Sand Bar Restaurant.

Sam, though frightened, did not understand the impact of the event. I overheard one person say that it was a lot of energy and time and money invested just to look for one child. But Jesus would disagree. Jesus wants to reclaim everyone who is lost.

That is what the cross says to us. There is no length to which God will not go to rescue one solitary soul. And when that one lost person is found all of heaven rejoices.

This brings us to the next thing we need to recognize: we are the lost sheep, we are the lost coin. It is our tendency to think of lost people as the homeless, the addicted, the person behind bars. Brothers and sisters, we are that lost person if we have never opened ourselves fully to the love of Jesus Christ. We are the lost sheep, we are the lost coin. We are Sam wandering down the beach.

Luke 15:1–10

He's Your Brother

Jesus was telling this parable to a crowd that included scribes and Pharisees, as well as sinners and tax-collectors. Jesus wanted them to see that none of them had an exclusive claim on the kingdom of God. We are all sinners saved by grace. Consequently, we dare not look down on anyone else. Each of us is precious to God and so is everyone else on earth. That makes us brothers and sisters, whoever we may be, whatever our rank or station.

There is a wonderful story about a young man named Billy who was attending his first day in Middle School.

At an opening assembly there was an introduction of all the homeroom teachers. Miss Smith was introduced first. She was an "easy" teacher, so the kids cheered as she was introduced. Mr. Brown was next and he also met with thundering approval.

Next was Mr. Johnson who was known to be a very strict disciplinarian. The kids loudly jeered most unkindly when his name was called. The pain was evident on his face.

This scene was devastating to young Billy. He was a sensitive kid and he could not believe how the other students were treating this Mr. Johnson. Suddenly he stood up in the middle of the bleachers and shouted: "Shut up everyone! That's my father!" Instantly, the jeering and the booing stopped.

After school, Billy went home. When he saw his real father, he began to cry. "Dad, I told a lie at school today," Billy said. He told his dad about the incident and how he had said that Mr. Johnson was his father and how he had yelled at all the other kids to "shut up" and be nice to the man.

His dad said: "It's all right, son. You just got the family members mixed up. Mr. Johnson's not your father, he's your brother."

Unexpected Grace

A story is told about Fiorello La Guardia, who, when he was mayor of New York City during the worst days of the Great Depression and all of WWII, was called by adoring New Yorkers the Little Flower because he always wore a carnation in his lapel. He was a colorful character who used to ride the New York City fire trucks, raid speakeasies with the police department, take entire orphanages to baseball games, and whenever the New York newspapers were on strike, he would go on the radio and read the Sunday funnies to the kids.

One bitterly cold night in January of 1935, the mayor turned up at a night court that served the poorest ward of the city. LaGuardia dismissed the judge for the evening and took over the bench himself.

Within a few minutes, a tattered old woman was brought before him, charged with stealing a loaf of bread. She told LaGuardia that her daughter's husband had deserted her, her daughter was sick, and her two grandchildren were starving. But the shopkeeper, from whom the bread was stolen, refused to drop the charges.

"It's a real bad neighborhood, your Honor," the shopkeeper told the mayor. "She's got to be punished to teach other people around here a lesson."

LaGuardia sighed. He turned to the woman and said, "I've got to punish you. The law makes no exceptions. I fine you ten dollars or ten days in jail."

But even as he pronounced sentence, the mayor was already reaching into his pocket. He extracted a bill and tossed it into his famous sombrero saying: "Here is the ten dollar fine which I now remit; and furthermore I am going to fine everyone in this courtroom fifty cents for living in a town where a person has to steal bread so that her grandchildren can eat.

In that courtroom everyone paid up and $47.50 was collected for the bewildered old lady who had stolen a loaf of bread to feed her starving grandchildren."

The musical *Les Miz* had obviously not yet opened on Broadway, but the mayor had certainly heard the story.

Unexpected grace. Unexpected grace is what our Gospel lesson for today is all about.

Matthew 21:23–32

Don't Be in Such a Hurry

Almost every person's most common complaint about life is that there just is not enough time. I read about a young wife who called a newspaper office and asked for the food editor. She needed an answer from an authority.

"Would you please help me?" she asked frantically. "I'm cooking a special dinner tonight for my husband's boss and his wife. I've never cooked a big dinner before, and I want everything to be perfect. I bought a nine-pound turkey. Could you tell me how long to cook it in my new microwave?"

"Just a minute," the food editor said, as she turned to check her reference book.

"Oh, thank you," the young wife said. "You've been a big help. Good-bye!"

A Fourth of July Story

For freedom Christ has set us free.

Paul was so confident in his love for the Lord that he had no fear. Even when his captors threatened him, his trust in God surpassed any fear.

You cannot enslave a person if they are so committed to an idea or a cause that fear has become inconsequential.

Our flag is the sign of our freedom. Many people have fought for that flag. You may have heard it before but good stories are worth hearing again.

Lt. Commander Mike Christian was a prisoner of war for years during the Viet Nam War. Mike had collected scraps of white and red cloth, and had sewn the scraps into stars and stripes which he then sewed to the inside of his blue pajama top to form an American flag.

The men would hang Mike's pajama top on a wall each night and say the pledge of allegiance to it. It was a ritual that brought them all together and reminded them of their purpose.

One day, the guards happened to catch the men saying the pledge. They dragged Mike away, took his pajamas, and beat him brutally. But that very night when Mike was returned to his cell, he began gathering little scraps of cloth again. He was already starting on another flag.

Mike had no fear. The apostle Paul had no fear. Throughout all the hardship, Paul lived as Christ lived, by the fruits of the Holy Spirit, which are: *"love, joy, peace, patience, kindness, generosity, faithfulness, gentleness and self-control."*

With his commitment to Christ, Paul let go of fear and gained freedom. It has to do with having courage.

The freedom is for each of us for *"if we live by the Spirit, we will be guided by the Spirit."*

Pay Better Attention

Do we truly pay attention when dealing with one another?

A man says that he and his wife were snuggled together on the floor one chilly evening watching television.

During a commercial break, he says she reached over and gave his foot a gentle squeeze.

"M-m-m-m-m," he said. "That's so nice."

"Actually," his wife admitted sheepishly, "I thought your foot was the remote."

Luke 15:1–10
God Will Not Stop

There is a wonderful story about the late author and poet Maya Angelou. I love this story for it shows so clearly that if we are just a tiny little sheep that has lost his way God will find a way to find us.

Maya wrote that years ago when she first came to San Francisco as a young woman she became 'sophisticated.' She said that was what you were supposed to do when you go to San Francisco, you become 'sophisticated.'

And for that reason she said she became agnostic. She thought the two went together. She said that it wasn't that she stopped believing in God, just that God no longer frequented the neighborhoods that she frequented.

She could do it all on her own. She didn't have to have God in her life anymore.

She was taking voice lessons at the time. Her teacher gave her an exercise where she was to read out of some religious pamphlet. The reading ended with these words: "God loves me."

She finished the reading, put the pamphlet down. The teacher said, "I want you to read that last sentence again."

So she picked it up, read it again, "God loves me." This time she read it somewhat sarcastically before put it down again.

The teacher said, "Read it again."

She read it again.

Then she described what happened. "After about the seventh repetition I began to sense there might be some truth in this statement. That there was a possibility that God really loves me, Maya Angelou.

"I suddenly began to cry at the grandness of it all. I knew if God loved me, I could do wonderful things. I could do great things. I could learn anything. I could achieve anything. For what could stand against me with God, since one person, any person, with God forms a majority now."

Maya was an active member of Glide Memorial United Methodist Church in San Francisco when she died.

We are like that in many ways, aren't we? If we are lost in any way, no matter how long we have been lost, God will not stop until we are found just like the woman who would not stop sweeping her house until she found that coin. Just like the shepherd even with ninety-nine other sheep to care for, stops and finds us.

When Ever I Am Weak, This I Am Strong

Retired seminary professor Fred Craddock tells a most memorable story about a pastor he met who had been born with no arms. This pastor described to Craddock how difficult it was as a child to put on his own clothes without any arms. He said his mother always dressed him, and he'd gotten to be a pretty big boy. She fed him, she dressed him. But one day she put his clothes in the middle of the floor and said to her armless child, "You need to learn to dress yourself."

The boy said, "I can't dress myself, I don't have . . ."

She said, "You'll have to dress yourself," and she left the room.

He said, "I kicked, screamed, kicked, screamed, yelled, 'You don't love me anymore!'"

Finally, he realized that if he were to get any clothes on, he'd have to do it himself. After almost an hour of struggle, he finally got some clothes on.

He said, "It was not until later that I learned that during that time my mother was in the next room crying."

God does not cause our suffering, God shares our suffering when we have a thorn in the flesh. Is it a mere coincidence that when Christ hung on the cross, his head was crowned with thorns?

In the Stillness of Silence

This is a wonderful story of a woman named Mary Ann Bird. Mary Ann writes:

"I grew up knowing I was different, and I hated it. I was born with a cleft palate, and when I started school, my classmates made it clear to me how I must look to others: a girl with a misshapen lip, crooked nose, lopsided teeth and garbled speech.

"When schoolmates would ask, 'What happened to your lip?' I'd tell them I'd fallen and cut it on a piece of glass. Somehow it seemed more acceptable to have suffered an accident than to have been born different. I was convinced that no one outside my family could love me.

"There was, however, a teacher in the second grade that we all adored – Mrs. Leonard. She was a happy lady, a sparkling lady. Each year, we would take a hearing test. I was virtually deaf in one of my ears; but when I had taken the test in past years, I discovered that if I did not press my hand as tightly upon my ear as I was instructed to do, I could pass the test.

"Mrs. Leonard gave the test to everyone in the class, and finally it was my turn. I knew from past years that as we stood and covered one ear, the teacher at the desk would whisper something and we would have to repeat it back . . . things like, 'The sky is blue' or Do you have new shoes?'

"I waited for the words and listened and listened. Then I heard seven words which changed my life. Then in the stillness of silence, Mrs. Leonard said, in her whisper, as I listened: 'I wish you were my little girl.'"

He Kept the Faith

The Second Letter of Paul to Timothy suggests that Paul is in prison or at least under house arrest in Rome. He is abandoned by all but a few of his friends and is now facing imminent death. Yes, the end is near for Paul. This was not just a guess; it was a certainty. He was under no illusion about his fate. So it was that he took pen in hand and wrote a parting letter to his friend and close associate Timothy. He writes: *"I have fought the good fight, I have finished the race, I have kept the faith."*

Now, why does Paul look back on such a life as a success? He succeeded because he kept the faith.

In the Broadway play *The Miracle Worker*, we learn the story of Ann Sullivan, the woman who taught Helen Keller how to communicate. It was during the 1890's, in the hills of northern Alabama, when she struggled with Helen and her handicaps - deaf, blind, and mute. Helen Keller was the miracle, but Ann Sullivan was the miracle worker.

What was the quality that marked Ann Sullivan's life? Was it that she fought a good fight? Clearly she did.

It is hard for us to even imagine not only the primitive care and the prejudices of that day, but also the fact that Helen's parents saw their child as a hopeless case.

Was the quality that marked her life that she finished the race? Clearly she did that as well. Ann Sullivan went on when most everyone else would have given up.

Her reward? Her student Helen Keller received the PhD from Temple University in Philadelphia and became an inspiration for thousands. The thing that most distinguished Ann Sullivan's life, however, is that she kept the faith. Throughout it all she kept believing.

A great life lesson from Paul's experience is that it's not what happens to us that counts, but how we respond to what happens to us. And Paul did handle his life, because he kept the faith.

The Light of the World Has Come and It Is Jesus

When Tom was a teenager, he and his friends were walking around the neighborhood one evening. It was a warm night and very dark. Suddenly one of them saw a police car. They had not done anything wrong, but they panicked and began to run.

The policemen saw them run and watched them turn down an alley. Tom tripped and knocked over some trash cans. The police officers got out of the car and began chasing after them. One of the officers turned on a searchlight. Tom looked around for his friends, but didn't see them. All he saw was that burning, searing searchlight, looking for him. Tom jumped behind the trash cans, only to find his friends huddled there.

They frantically began pulling trash over their heads and trying to hide. But their attempt to hide didn't work. The spotlight fell on Tom.

"Come out where we can see you," said the voice behind the light. Tom stood up where he was, covered with garbage.

"What are you doing here?" said the voice.

Tom stammered in a whisper, "Nothing."

The voice said, "I can't hear you. What are you doing?"

Tom said, "Officer, I wasn't doing anything wrong. I saw the police car and got scared and ran. I accidentally knocked over these garbage cans. I'm sorry about the disturbance."

The searchlight was beaming into his eyes, partially blinding him. He stood there in the light covered in leftover food and garbage with nowhere to hide.

Then the Officer said, "I think I recognize you. Don't you live around the corner?"

"Yes," Tom stammered. His heart was racing, and he said, "Please Officer, don't arrest me. My life will be ruined. I'll never get into law school. It will be bad enough when my parents find out!"

But then the officer behind the light said something totally unexpected, "Son, never run from a policeman. I'm not here to punish you; I'm here to protect you."

As he stood before that searchlight, Tom caught a glimpse of what it means to stand before Jesus, who is the Light of the World. There he was, fully exposed; yet completely protected. He was fully revealed, yet free from unnecessary punishment. He stood hip-deep in garbage, yet cleaner than he had ever felt, somehow cleansed by a light that cast no shadow.

In that moment, he felt something of what it means to stand in the presence of Jesus, who is full of truth and full of grace.

"I am the light of the world," says Jesus. *"Whoever follows me will never walk in darkness but will have the light of life."*

2 Corinthians 12:2-10

To The Utter Surprise

How can this be? How can Paul's weaknesses, insults, hardships, persecutions and difficulties be a blessing? How can these "thorns of the flesh" be turned into blessings?

For one thing, thorns can give us empathy for others.

A few years ago there was a movie starring Harrison Ford titled, *Regarding Henry*. It was the story of Henry Turner, a successful Manhattan-based attorney who seems to have everything: a perfect wife, a perfect daughter, a perfect life.

However, this is just a façade. In reality, Henry's a despicable and ruthless trial lawyer, unfaithful to his wife and seemingly without regard to the well-being of those around him. No surprise that his family life is a mess.

But then one night he goes out to get a pack of cigarettes and he finds himself in the middle of a robbery that goes bad and he is shot in the head and chest. He survives the injury but with significant brain damage; he initially cannot move or talk or remember anyone or anything.

He has to go through months of rehabilitation and relearn everything: how to speak, walk, and function normally.

And yet it is in this time of immense struggle that Henry discovers how to love his family and friends again and how to find true happiness in life. He becomes a different human being, more caring and understanding and compassionate.

To the utter surprise of his wife and daughter, Henry becomes a loving and affectionate man.

No one would wish this kind of experience on any human being, yet Henry Turner would probably never have become an authentic human being without this experience.

And That Is Dying

This story has been told many times, at many funerals, but it never fails to bring comfort to those that hear it:

I am standing upon a seashore. A ship at my side spreads her white sails to the morning breeze and starts for the blue ocean. She is an object of beauty and strength and I stand and watch her until at length she hangs like a speck of white cloud just where the sea and sky come to mingle with each other.

Then someone at my side says, "There! She's gone."

Gone? Gone where? Gone from my sight, that is all. She is just as large in mast and hull and spar as she was when she left my side. And she is just as able to bear her load of living right to her destined port. Her diminished size is in me, not in her.

And just at that moment when someone at my side says, "There! She's gone," there are other eyes watching her coming and other voices ready to take up the glad shout, "Here she comes!"

And that is dying.

What Do You See?

A family was driving through Kansas on vacation. Five-year-old Tyler was looking out the car window. "Boy," he said, "it's so flat out there, you can look farther than you can see."

That's a great phrase - "you can look farther than you can see."

In the early 1930s an engineer named Joseph Strauss looked out over San Francisco Bay. In his mind he formed a picture of a beautiful bridge connecting the two sides of the bay.

In 1936 the Golden Gate Bridge became a reality. He had a vision. He looked farther than he could see.

The following is an example of "vision":

If there were a pile of scrap cardboard, old car parts, used tires, and other cast-offs, what would be the first thought that would pop into your mind? Trash heap. Junkyard. Eyesore.

Yet there was an article in *Time* magazine a few years back about a professor at Auburn University who looked at those same items and saw new homes.

Professor Samuel Mockbee is the visionary behind an architecture firm that specializes in making lovely, functional, low-cost public buildings and homes for poor residents in Alabama. Mockbee and his students make these lovely, functional buildings out of trash.

Specifically, they turn scrap cardboard, old car parts, used tires, and other cast-offs into real homes. Last year some of these students built a chapel and community center for the residents of Mason's Bend, a tiny, rural town.

The students used more than 100 discarded car windows to make one wall of the center. Former students have made homes out of hay bales or old tires. Some of these homes, which are donated to local residents, are attractive enough to be featured in architectural magazines. These students learn to see value in refuse, and to turn that refuse into something beautiful and lasting.

Some people look at discarded car windows and see trash. Others see building materials. The difference is vision.

What do you see? How you look at your world and how you look at yourself will determine to a great extent what you will contribute to the world and how great you will feel about your life.

Happy Endings

There is a story of a father who took his six-year-old son to a pet shop to pick out a puppy for his birthday present.

For over a half an hour the little boy looked at the assortment of puppies in the window.

"Have you decided which one you want?" asked his Daddy.

"Yes," the little fellow replied, pointing to the puppy that was enthusiastically wagging its tail. "I want the one with the happy ending."

A Story of Love

There is a beautiful story about the courtship of Moses Mendelssohn, the grandfather of the great German composer, Felix Mendelsshon.

Moses Mendelssohn was a small man with a misshapen, humped back. One day he visited a merchant in Hamburg who had a lovely daughter. Though Mendelssohn admired her greatly, she avoided him, seemingly afraid of his grotesque hump.

On the last day of his visit he went to tell her goodbye. Her face seemed to beam with beauty but when he entered, she cast her eyes to the floor.

Mendelssohn's heart ached for her. After some small talk, he slowly drew to the subject that filled his mind. "Do you believe that marriages are made in Heaven?" he asked.

"Yes," replied the young woman. "And do you?"

"Of course," Mendelssohn answered. "I believe that at the birth of each child, the Lord says, 'That boy shall marry that girl.' But in my case, the Lord also added, 'But alas, his wife will have a terrible hump.' At that moment I called, 'Oh Lord that would be a tragedy for her. Please give me the humped back and let her be beautiful.'"

We are told that the young woman was so moved by these words that she reached for Mendelssohn's hand and later became his loving and faithful wife.

John 20:1–8

Tears of Joy

Jesus said to her, *"Woman, why are you weeping?"*

Tears of joy are appropriate for Easter because they express our exhilaration of victory. The heavy stone of the tomb has been rolled away. Sorrow precedes joy; Easter follows Good Friday.

A minister preached at a prison where there were many life-term prisoners. While he was there, the Parole Board chose the occasion to release one of them.

The Warden announced that the prisoners could choose by secret ballot the one whom they thought worthy of release.

After the vote was taken, the Warden called out the name of the winner: Reuben Johnson. No one stood up. He said again, "Reuben Johnson, will you stand?" Every convict turned and looked at Johnson.

Reuben Johnson sat there with tears streaming down his face. He was too overcome to stand. He was free. He was forgiven. The reality of it all was beyond his comprehension and the only reaction he could make was to weep tears of joy.

When we are released from guilt and set free to be full and complete persons, with tears, we ask, "What did you find in me that you have dealt so lovingly with me?"

Then, rejoice people - rejoice as we celebrate that we have a living Christ who loves us and blesses us.

Be Kind to One Another

There is an organization in Hollywood, CA called The Holy Ghost Repair Service, Incorporated. And no, they aren't in the business of repairing shoes, watches, or automobiles. On their stationary they state as their purpose "repairing broken lives for Jesus . . . in the power of his Spirit."

We may express it a little less colorfully, but that is our church's purpose as well, "repairing broken lives for Jesus in the power of his Spirit."

Some of us know what it is to have broken lives. There is an old western legend about a rancher who was out riding and came upon a Native American friend of his lying flat on the ground with his ear pressed against the earth.

Without looking up the Indian said in broken English: "Wagon . . . wagon pulled by horses . . . two horses . . . man driving wagon . . . long beard . . . wearing buckskin . . . woman in wagon . . . dressed in calico . . . "

The rancher was amazed. "You can tell all of that just by pressing your ear to the ground?" he asked.

"No," grunted his friend. "The wagon ran over me 30 minutes ago."

Some of us have had those times in life when we've felt like a wagon has run over us, when we were in need of the Holy Ghost Repair Service. We give thanks that we have a comforter, a counselor, an unseen presence to see us through these times.

But the above scripture is not about those times when we feel like we've been run over by a wagon. It is about the other times, the times when we're tempted to run over others.

As Paul wrote to the Ephesians: *"Put away all bitterness and wrath and anger . . . be kind to one another . . . forgiving one another, as God in Christ has forgiven you."*

2 Corinthians 12:2–10

Mug Him Again

Former mayor of New York City Ed Koch used to tell a story about a judge who was the victim of a mugging. Afterward he held a news conference. In a formal and grave voice, the judge said, "This mugging will in no way affect my decisions in the courtroom in matters of this kind."

An elderly woman, with the rage of a victim glowing in her face, stood up in the back of the room and shouted, "Then mug him again!"

God doesn't mug us with pain and suffering in order to bring us closer to Him. Notice that St. Paul calls his thorn in the flesh "a messenger of Satan." It didn't come from God.

God was not seeking to get his attention through his discomfort, whatever that "thorn" might have been. But God could use his pain, his suffering to make him a stronger man. God could use his pain and suffering to make him a blessing to others. Therefore Paul could write: *"I delight in weaknesses, in insults, in hardships, in persecutions, in difficulties. For when I am weak, then I am strong."*

So Who Is The Greatest?

A funny thing happened on the way to Capernaum. A group of twelve grown men were arguing among themselves as to who was the greatest among them. These were not corporate executives . . . or football players . . . or candidates for President. They were men who had been chosen by God to be his intimate circle, to spread his good news, to proclaim to Israel that its redemption was at hand.

Mark gives no specific details of this incident but we can almost hear Andrew telling his brother Peter: "I saw him first, I introduced you to him. I am the greatest."

Peter retorts that he is the greatest for he is the one to whom the keys of the church are given.

Then John says it is James and he who are the greatest for Jesus always took them to the mountain to pray with him; they even met Moses and Elijah while they were there.

Judas even thinks he is the greatest for he is the one that takes care of the money.

The conversation must have sounded rather ridiculous: "I am the greatest." "No, I am the greatest." "No, me. I'm the greatest." "Me, me, me, I am the greatest."

Then they were stopped in their tracks when Jesus asked them what they had been arguing about. There was just silence; they were too embarrassed to admit what it was.

But of course Jesus knew.

How silly it was for men of such knowledge and faith to be arguing over something so trivial.

So, who is the greatest?

Is it Mohammed Ali? In 1964 upon winning the heavyweight boxing championship, he exclaimed to the world, "I am the greatest!" "I'm Number One!"

Or was the greatest among us the famous writer Ernest Hemingway who received a Pulitzer Prize?

Or Archbishop Desmond Tutu who received the Nobel Peace Prize?

Maybe it was Jonas Salk who put an end to polio or Michelangelo because of his incredible painting of the Sistine Chapel and his statue of David?

Or maybe, just maybe, the greatest is the young child that Jesus took into his arms.

Silent Tear

Each night we shed a silent tear,
   As we speak to you in prayer.
To let you know we love you,
   And just how much we care.
Take our million teardrops,
   Wrap them up in love,
Then ask the wind to carry them,
   To you in heaven above.

Matthew 4:19

Walk In His Footsteps

This story is adapted from the book *Life Rails: Holding Fast to God's Promise* by Scott Walker. Walker tells the true story of James Pierson, a friend of his who was a soldier during the Second World War.

Pierson was in charge of a reconnaissance team that was sent out to survey enemy lines. On one particular mission they had to cross an American mine field before they could get over into German territory. Fortunately the field was well marked for the American soldiers by little flags indicating the location of a mine. So very carefully they made their way through the booby- trapped terrain.

Just as they were safely across the field and nearly to the front lines they were pinned them down by German machine gun fire. The entire platoon of reconnaissance soldiers were stopped in their tracks. As time passed they realized that their position was precarious. The German army would be advancing soon. They realized that the only thing they could do was retreat and that meant going back across the mine field.

In the meantime, while they had been pinned down, snow had been falling for it was the middle of winter. By the time the decision was made to modify their mission and start back, enough snow had fallen to cover up the markers that denoted the placement of the mines.

The Lieutenant, acting quickly, called his men together and gave them this order: "I will go first across the field. You are to follow 30 yards apart. You are to walk in my footprints. That way if I hit a mine, I alone will be killed."

Keeping 30 yards distance between each other and walking exactly in the footprints of their leader, they miraculously made it back across the mine field safely. As the last soldier turned and looked at the line of footprints, it looked as if only one person had made the journey. They had followed exactly in the steps of their lieutenant.

Later some engineers came to re-mark the location of the mines. It appeared that on one step the soldiers had stepped right across a mine. They had just barely missed setting it off. But they all got back safely because they followed in the footsteps of their leader.

Is that not our hope as well? This is more than saying that Jesus is our example. He is that, but far, far more.

He is our Great High Priest. He is the one who has already passed through the heavens and now mediates in our behalf before the throne of God so that we might come confidently after Him, that by walking in his steps we will receive mercy and grace and help in our times of need.

Baby Questions to God

About four-years-ago a baby was heard asking God:

"They tell me you are sending my brother and me to earth tomorrow, but how are we going to live there being so small and helpless?"

God answered, "Your angel will be waiting for you and will take care of you."

The baby girl further inquired, "But tell me. Here in heaven we don't have to do anything but sing and smile and be happy. What will happen on earth?"

God said, "Your angel will sing for you and will also smile for you. And you will feel your angel's love and be very happy."

Now the boy child asked, "And how are we going to be able to understand when people talk to us if we don't know the language?"

God said, "Your angel will tell you the most beautiful and sweet words you will ever hear, and with much patience and care, your angel will teach you how to speak."

And what are we going to do when we want to talk to you?"

God said, "Your angel will place your hands together and will teach you how to pray."

"Who will protect us?"

God said, "Your angel will defend you even if it means risking her life."

"But we will always be sad because we will not see you anymore."

God said, "Your angel will always talk to you about Me and will teach you the way to come back to Me, even though I will always be next to you."

At that moment there was much peace in Heaven, but voices from Earth could be heard and the children hurriedly asked, "God, if we are to leave now, please tell us our angel's name.

"You will simply call her 'Mommy'."

"But, God, there are two of us. Can one angel take care of us both?"

God answered, "There will be another angel to help her."

"What will we call that angel?"

"Daddy."

Happy Mother's Day . . . and

Father's Day (next month)!

The Persistence of Faith

And then Jesus looked at her and opened himself to her and said, *"Woman, great is your faith! Let it be done for you as you wish."* The daughter was healed instantly.

This reminds me of an experience I had at Jackson Memorial Hospital a few years ago. In the Spinal Injury unit was a girl named Maria. Maria was a beautiful 12-year-old Filipino who along with her three cousins and aunt and uncle had been on their way to Disney World. The van her uncle was driving had a tire blow out and her uncle lost control and wrecked. The uncle and one cousin were killed.

Maria survived the crash but she was unable to breathe on her own. She lived with a tracheotomy and a respirator breathing for her. She lived unable to speak or communicate in any way. Moreover, it was determined that the accident left her with no eyesight.

She had been in a coma for several months when I first saw her. But during the time since the accident the family's faith in God had never faltered. Maria's parents were faithful in prayer while diligently watching over their daughter day and night. A common sight would be to see them running after a doctor to beg him or her to talk to them, grabbing hold of the sleeve of the doctor's coat. "Please give us some hope for Maria" was their plea. The mother was constantly approaching all the health care providers asking them to help Maria.

After much treatment and a thorough review of Maria's case, the doctors told the family that there was no hope for Maria and it had been decided that the respirator should be turned off.

But it seemed like each time the physician started to approach the turning off of the respirator, something would happen and the decision would be delayed.

Friends and family members also had begun keeping a faithful and prayerful watch in Maria's room. Out of this faithfulness, many other people were touched. The nurses and physical therapists started to pray.

One day when I was with a patient on another wing of the hospital, he asked me if I knew Maria and if I would tell her parents that he and his roommates were praying for her. This man was paralyzed from the waist down because of a drunken driver accident.

During a prayer service, special prayers were given for Maria. And even a few doctors were there praying for her.

Some time past, Maria was taken off the respirator, began breathing on her own and was discharged from the hospital. Living with her family at home, Maria started to gradually come out of the coma and began to communicate with her family.

The persistence of faith prevailed.

She Witnessed
The Love of Christ
By How She Lived

In 1921, Lewis Lawes was the warden at Sing Sing Prison, the toughest prison in the country at that time. Twenty years after Lawes became warden, the prison had become a model humanitarian institution. Many studied his system, but Lawes gave the credit to his wife Catherine, who is buried near the prison gates.

Catherine Lawes was a mother with three small children when her husband was appointed warden. Everybody warned her that she should never ever set foot inside the prison walls, but that did not stop Catherine!

When the first prison basketball game was held, she went . . . she walked into the gym with her three children and sat in the stand with the inmates. Her parents and friends could not believe that she wanted to get acquainted with the inmates.

One day, she learned that a convicted murderer was blind. Holding his hand in hers, she asked, "Do you read Braille?"

"What's Braille?" asked the inmate.

Catherine taught herself Braille and then she taught the prisoner how to read.

There was a deaf man in prison. Catherine went to school to learn how to use sign language and to teach him.

Catherine was the body of Jesus that came alive again and again over the years in Sing Sing Prison.

Then one day, Catherine was killed in a car accident. The following day, her body was resting in a casket in her home, three-quarters of a mile from the prison.

As the second-in-command and acting-warden took his early morning walk, he was shocked to see a large crowd of the toughest, hardest-looking criminals gathered at the main gate. He came closer and saw tears of grief and sadness. He knew how much they loved Catherine.

He turned and faced them and said, "All right men, you can go see her. Just be sure to check back in tonight!" Then he opened the gate and a parade of the hardest core criminals walked through the gate of the prison, without chains, without a guard. They walked the three-quarters of a mile to stand in line to pay their final respects to Catherine Lawes.

And by that night every one of them had checked back into the prison. They were deeply touched by the Christ-like qualities of Catherine and the trust of the assistant warden.

Catherine Lawes witnessed the love of Christ by how she lived. And the hardest of the hard responded to her.

Reconciliation Day

One Sunday afternoon, my husband Phil and I drove down to Miami to be with my friend Caroline while she died. Two days later, at Caroline's funeral, one of her daughters said that her mother had so emptied herself that the light of Christ shone through her. Without a doubt, Caroline died right with our Lord.

I want to die right with God. We all want to die right with God. To be right with God I, we, must have made every effort to be right with others. It is incredible how giving forgiveness to someone or seeking forgiveness from someone unloads the gun in the other person's hand.

Here is an interesting letter to advice columnist Ann Landers. It deals with handling anger and resentment.

"Dear Ann,

"I've suddenly become aware that the years are flying by. Time somehow seems more precious. My parents suddenly seem old. My aunts and uncles are sick. I haven't seen some of my cousins for several years. I love my family Ann, but we've grown apart. Now my thoughts have turned to the dark side. I remember the feelings I've hurt, and I recall my own hurt feelings from the misunderstandings and un-mended fences that separated us and set up barriers.

"I think of my mother and her sister, who haven't spoken to each other in five years. As a result of that argument, my cousin and I haven't spoken either. What a waste of precious time.

"Wouldn't it be terrific if a special day could be set aside to reach out and make amends? We could call it "Reconciliation Day." Everyone would vow to write a letter or make a phone call and mend a strained or broken

relationship. It could also be the day on which we would all agree to accept the olive branch extended by a relative or a former friend. This day could be the starting place. We could go on from there to heal the wounds in our hearts and rejoice in a brand new beginning.
[signed] Van Nuys."

I don't know if "Reconciliation Day" ever got off the ground, but it is certainly a great idea. Reconciliation is at the heart of Christian faith. Paul writes in II Corinthians, *"All this is from God, who reconciled us to himself through Christ and gave us the ministry of reconciliation . . ."*

That is who we are. We are a reconciling community. Christ has reconciled us with God. We, then, are to be reconciled with one another.

Brothers and sisters, if the Lord Jesus can forgive us and make things right with us, how can we NOT do the same for others?

Forgiveness

This Old Testament scripture is about Joseph forgiving his brothers after the terrible way they treated him. The New Testament scripture is also about forgiveness. Peter is coming to Jesus asking if there is a cap on how often one has to forgive.

In a church other than ours, the Sunday School teacher had just told the story about Jericho and then addressed the class, "Class, who knocked down the wall of Jericho?"

No one answered, so she called on Colby. "Colby, tell me who knocked down the wall of Jericho?"

"Why are you asking me? I didn't do it and I don't know who did; and besides, if I did know, I don't rat on my friends," was his reply.

The teacher became very concerned about Colby's response and marched him right out the classroom and down to the Sunday School Superintendent's office. "Mr. Superintendent, Colby refuses to tell me who broke down the wall of Jericho. He is making a joke of it. He should be disciplined."

The superintendent replied, "Let's all calm down. If something on the church grounds has been broken, it's a matter for the vestry to investigate. Don't worry. We will take care of it."

Now, obviously everybody missed the point, but Colby needed to know, and we all need to know, that there is forgiveness even if we knock down the walls of Jericho.

Unresolved Anger

Anger is most destructive when it is allowed to lie dormant for a long time and fester like an infected wound.

In his book, *The Great Divorce*, C.S. Lewis tells the story of a visitor who is permitted to be a temporary guest in hell. At one point, the visitor accompanies a busload of souls from hell who are allowed to visit heaven. While in heaven these residents of hell each have the privilege of staying in heaven if they choose. Surprisingly, they do not choose to do so.

The book considers the stories of these passengers, telling why they would rather not stay in heaven! One of these is a woman whose husband had treated her shabbily on earth. She decides to return to hell. The reason is she would rather burn in hell than forgive her husband.

Tragedy so often results from unresolved anger and resentment. Remember the old adage: never let the sun set on your anger. It is a good principle for everyone concerned. It's good for your marriage, your family, your heart, your health, your business, and your relationships.

Luke 10:1–12, 16–20
Travel Light

In the great book, *The Cost of Discipleship*, Dietrich Bonhoeffer writes that Jesus' call to travel light may be a call to simplify our lives "to become more carefree" so we can regain a kind of "singleness of eye and heart." The disciples needed this singleness of eye and heart to do the mission as Christ told them. We need that singleness of eye and heart.

What is all the stuff that bogs us down? What excess baggage do we carry? Emotional baggage might be all that resentment, anger and hurt that we just won't let go of. Physical baggage is all that stuff, be it clothes, cars, houses or other possessions that get in the way of us following Jesus.

Healing often has to do with unpacking or "shedding" all those things that weigh us down. Healing is accepting Jesus' invitation to send us out as his missionaries, to fall in love again with our life of faith, to follow Jesus again with a light step and light heart, a little courage for the rough spots, prayers, a skip and a song. To travel light.

Today airline's charge for an extra bag has made us more aware of how little we need to pack. I remember when I went on a mission trip to Kenya while I was in seminary. We were told we could bring one small suitcase. One suitcase for the whole summer! You know what, I was so glad I did. Because it freed me to use my time not to worry about my clothes but how I was with others in my heart. When it was time to return home, we were asked to leave our belongings with those Africans who needed them much more than we did. I came home with a very light suitcase.

We are to be free from excessive baggage. Jesus wants us to trust that God will provide for us wherever our life's journey may take us. And that involves trusting beyond understanding.

Matthew 15:21–28

More Than One Way To Take Care of It

Now there was once an old reprobate who had lived a wild and loose life, too much in love with the bad side of living. When he died the local minister, who was something of a tyrant, insisted that the man be buried outside the fence of the church cemetery. The consecrated ground inside the fence was for only good and upstanding Christians.

Years later the minister was long gone and the man's daughter came to the church to pay her respects. But she could not find the grave outside of the fence. She went over to the caretaker and asked him what had happened to her father's grave, "Had someone moved it?"

The caretaker smiled and said, "Oh, it's right there. We didn't move your father's grave . . . We moved the fence."

I Love You
With All My Heart

If we say to someone, "I love you with all my heart," we are saying, "I am committed to you. All that I have is yours. I trust you enough that I am willing to share with you everything I have, everything I am, and everything I hope to be." That kind of commitment is what God asks of us as well. For truly it is all His in the first place.

There is a bitter-cute story going around that makes a powerful point about where too many of we Christians are right now. According to the story, the Pope needed a heart transplant. There was much concern throughout the Roman Catholic world; from where would the new heart come?

Thousands of people had gathered outside of the Vatican yelling and waving their hands and calling out, "Take my heart, Papa, take my heart!"

Well, the Pope didn't know what to do, but an idea popped into his head. He asked everyone to please be quiet for a few minutes and he told them that he was going to throw down a feather. Upon whomever the feather landed, he would take their heart for the transplant.

The Pope then threw the feather down from his balcony and upon the people. Suddenly everyone stopped yelling and waving their hands. Instead they were leaning their heads back and blowing the feather back into the air and moving out of the way of the feather to make sure it didn't land on them.

God deserves everything we have, everything we are, everything we hope to be. Render unto Caesar the things that are Caesar's and unto God the things that are God's. We live in the United States, the greatest country the world has ever known. We are citizens of this land but we are first and foremost citizens of heaven.

Every time you walk into a church you see the cross and are reminded that the reason you are to give to God the things that are God's is because God has already given you everything.

Matthew 4:1–11

Temptation of the Devil

The great theologian Martin Luther was asked how he overcomes the temptation of the devil.

He replied, "Well, when he comes knocking at the door of my heart, and asks, 'Who lives here?' I don't rush to answer but allow the dear Lord Jesus to go to the door and say, 'Martin Luther used to live here, but he has moved out. I, the Lord Jesus Christ, live here now.'"

All the King's Horses and All the King's Men

Humpty Dumpty sat on a wall.
Humpty Dumpty had a great fall.
All the King's horses and all the King's men
Couldn't put Humpty Dumpty back together again.
Wait a minute . . . this can't end like this. All the King's horses and all the King's men couldn't put Humpty back together again? What about the King? Couldn't he put Humpty together again?

Let's continue with this wonderful Nursery Rhyme.

I think that as soon as the King heard of Humpty's fate, he was greatly disturbed. So, setting aside his royal finery, disguised as a common peasant, the King slipped unnoticed through the majestic palace gates and into the rough-and-tumble street life of his kingdom.

The King meandered through the back streets and alleys in search of Humpty. After several days and nights the persistent monarch finally found him. Humpty's shattered body was scattered over a ten-foot circle amidst the broken glass and flattened beer cans of a back alley.

Though weak from searching, the King was overjoyed at the sight of Humpty. He ran to his side and cried, "Humpty! It is I - your King! I have powers greater than those of my horses and men who failed to put you back together again. Be at peace. I am here to help!"

"Leave me alone," Humpty's mouth retorted. "I've gotten used to this new way of life. I kind of like it now."

"But" was all the King could get out before Humpty continued. "I tell you, I'm fine. I like it here. That trash can over there...the way the sun sparkles on the broken glass. This must be the garden spot of the world!"

The King tried again, "I assure you my kingdom has more to offer than this back alley - there are green mountains, beautiful beaches, exciting cities . . ." But Humpty would hear none of it. And the saddened King returned to the palace.

A week later one of Humpty's eyes rolled skyward only to see once again the concerned face of the King standing over his shattered pieces. "I've come back to help," firmly stated the King.

"Look leave me alone, pal, will you?" said Humpty. "I've just seen my psychiatrist, and he assures me that I'm doing a fine job of coping with my environment as it is. You're the one who is a cop-out. A man has to deal with life as it comes. I'm a realist."

"But wouldn't you rather walk than just lie there?" asked the puzzled King.

"Look," Humpty's mouth replied, "once I get up and start walking I'll have to stay up and keep walking. At this point in my life I'm not ready to make a commitment like that. So, if you'll excuse me - you're blocking my sun."

Reluctantly the King turned once again and walked back through the streets of his kingdom to the palace.

But after a while, Humpty began to miss the visits of the King and waited and watched for his return. He waited and waited and waited for the King to come back. Actually, it was over a year before the King ventured out to see Humpty again. Humpty was very tired of the waiting.

But sure enough, one bright morning one of Humpty's ears that was lying over by an empty wine bottle perked up at the sure, steady strides of the King. This time

Humpty was ready. He couldn't wait for the King to get in earshot!

Humpty's eye turned toward the tall figure just as his mouth managed the words, "My King!"

Immediately the King fell to his knees on the glass-covered pavement. His strong knowing hands gently began to piece together Humpty's shattered body. After some time, his work completed, the King rose to full height, pulling up with him the figure of a strong young man.

The two walked side by side through the kingdom. Together they stood atop lush green mountains. They ran together along the beaches. They laughed together as they strolled the gleaming cities of the King's domain. This went on forever. And to the depth, breadth and height of their friendship, there was no end.

Once while walking together down the sidewalk in one of the King's cities, Humpty overheard a remark that made his heart leap with joy.

He overheard someone ask, "Say, who are those two?"

Another replied, "Why the one on the left is old Humpty Dumpty. He sure looks different. I don't know the one on the right - but they certainly look like they are brothers!"

Matthew 2:1–12
The Beatitudes

A Sunday School teacher asked her young scholars if anyone could tell the class what the Beatitudes are. While the rest of the class thought about the possible answer, little Suzy, raised her hand excitedly, fairly bursting with the answer. "Oh, teacher, I know, I know! The Beatitudes are the attitudes we ought to be at!"

Rejoice and be glad, for your reward is great in heaven.

Mother Teresa of Calcutta felt rewarded constantly. Her whole life was rooted in the beatitudes of Jesus. Her caring service toward the poorest of the poor of the world was in total imitation of Jesus' kindness and compassion. Even the non-Christians looked up to Mother Teresa and saw her as something like God. A dying beggar after being rescued in the streets of Calcutta, asked Mother Teresa, "Are you something like God?"

"No," she answered. "I am trying to be something like Jesus, the Son of God."

A Christmas Gift

A wife gave her husband two ties for Christmas. He, being an obedient and peace-loving man, went immediately and put on one of the ties. He returned to the kitchen where his wife was preparing breakfast.

Seeing he had on one of the ties she asked, "What's the matter, don't you like the other tie?"

The Joy of the Unexpected

As many of you know, my sister Esther died not too long ago. I had just visited her in Modesto, California two weeks before her death. She was in a place where she had no visitors so when the nurse opened the door and Esther saw me, her face lit up with the unexpected joy of surprise.

On my last day there, I wanted to celebrate her birthday which would be on the next Monday. I had noticed in my route from the motel to the mental health facility that there was a place called, "The Cheesecake Bakery." My first thought was only in California would there be something so specialized and that it was probably health-food cheesecake. I remembered those childhood times when we would walk five miles to a Jewish deli in Miami for cheesecake. So I stopped and got her a piece of cheesecake and a birthday card.

We were sitting in the garden together visiting and I took out the cheesecake. Her affect changed to the joy of surprise again and she said how this was so unexpected.

When I heard one evening when I was back home that her health was failing, I went into my little meditation room, lit a candle and opened up my Book of Common Prayer to page 462 and prayed the Litany at the Time of Death.

Several hours later when I learned she had died, I returned to my meditation room, lit a brand new candle, and prayed the Burial of the Dead service, also in our prayer book.

I savored the wonderful verse in the 21st chapter of The Revelation to John of how God will wipe away every tear and there shall be an end to death, and mourning and crying and pain will be no more; that all things will be made new. I then read the Gospel of John, the gospel cited above, and noticed how firmly Martha said, *"Lord, I do believe you are the Messiah, the Son of God."*

After this, as I was still in prayer, I was given an image: It was of God with arms wide open and there was Esther walking toward God. She looked up and with so much surprising joy and said, "This is all so unexpected!"

There is no doubt that Martha and Mary and others felt that joy of the unexpected the day when Lazarus walked out of the tomb. Remember the next time you cry when someone you love dies, that Jesus wept and weeping can be a sign of strength, instead of weakness.

Weeping can be a sign of faith, rather than a sign of fear. Our tears may be an indication that we are strong enough in our faith to accept the full implications of the tragedy. We dare not despair when we have nothing to hope for in the future.

The next time you feel like weeping, don't brush away those tears too rapidly. There is, in this life, "a time for tears." And there will be a time for each of us to die to this life. And that is when we will all have the joy of the unexpected.

Remember Jesus tells us: *"I am the resurrection and the life. Those who believe in me, even though they die, will live, and everyone who believes in me will never die."* This is our promise.

Christ, the Beacon of Light

In 1991, Robyn Stevens of Hancock, Maine, pondered over what she should give her father, Arthur, for Christmas. Her grandmother talked about the usefulness of flashlights. So, she bought a three-celled, waterproof flashlight from Sears. Her father was delighted.

The following month, Arthur was thirty-five miles out to sea in the Gulf of Maine. He was on the tugboat Harkness along with his two crew members. They were on their way home from a construction job. Halfway home, the crew found themselves in a nightmare. A severe storm was approaching. The temperature dropped drastically and the sky got very dark. The winds were at twenty-five knots and the wind chill factor was minus sixty degrees.

A little after 6 pm, the Captain checked the stern of the boat, only to discover they were taking on water. The tugboat was pitching violently and the decks were sheer ice. He radioed the Coast Guard station in Southwest Harbor and yelled, "Mayday! Mayday! We're going down. Help us."

The tugboat Harkness was sinking just off Matinicus Island where a handful of families lived during the winter. Vance Bunker was at home and heard the radio conversations between the Harkness and Coast Guard and knew that the three men did not stand a chance if they weren't rescued soon.

He and two other lobstermen left their families and set out to sea in the JanEllen, a thirty-six foot lobster boat. The sky was so cloudy and their windshield was so iced-up, they could not see one thing. All they could do was forge ahead in the darkness in faith.

At 7:01 pm Bunker heard what would be the last radio transmission from the Harkness. "The water is up to our chests in the wheelhouse," The Captain reported, "We're going into the water. God save us."

Bunker and his crew heard nothing after that except the roar of the wind and the creaking of their boat as it crashed through the waves. The possibility that three sailors had drowned brought a sickening feeling to the lobstermen's stomachs.

Shortly thereafter, one of the men on the JanEllen saw a small thin bead of light, pointing straight up. It was barely visible.

"Look, over there. Follow that light!"

Bunker turned the boat in the direction of the light and there they found three, nearly half-dead men with arms hooked together. Their clothes were frozen to a ladder that had come loose from the Harkness as she went down.

Arthur was closest to death and had lost his ability to hold on. But the freezing cold had done the men an odd turn. Frozen to the back of one of the men's gloves was a three-celled, waterproof flashlight. It was aiming straight up in the darkness. It had become a beacon for those who had enough faith to follow it.

Allow Christ to be your beacon of light, have faith, no matter what the darkness is you face. Do not fear any darkness. Jesus has come to be your light and that light will never fade or dim. This is your promise.

I Corinthian 3:10-11

Under Construction

When I was walking the 21-mile Big Sur Marathon walk a number of years ago, I could not help but notice that there were so many different sayings that people print on T-shirts and other things ... from advertisements to obscenities to affirmations of faith.

The most touching was the one that honored those that had been killed and maimed at the Boston Marathon two weeks before. Many of the runners run both the Boston and the Big Sur marathons the same month. They are called Coast to Coast Marathoners and proudly wore t-shirts proclaiming the same.

I even saw a t-shirt with the words Christian Under Construction printed on it. We can all appreciate what is meant by that. We can talk about the difference faith in Christ makes in our lives and about how it works and about examples of the new life in Christ that we have already experienced. Yet most of us know that we are not yet what God wants us to be.

At our best, we are Christians under construction. And, that is all right. That is a good way to be. The changes that God makes in our lives don't happen all at once. It is a good thing to know that we are in the process of becoming what God wants us to be and to participate in that process very intentionally and joyfully. We are heading in the right direction.

Sirach 40:12

Have Faith

Getting gas for the car the other day reminded me of the story of the nun in her car on her way to a much desired mission assignment at an Apache Indian Reservation. She was so excited that she drove past the last gas station without noticing she needed gas. And wouldn't you know it, she ran out of gas about a mile down the road, and had to walk back to the station. The station had gas, but the attendant said he had just sold his last container to hold the gas.

Sympathetic to her plight, he offered to search through an old shed in the back for something that might suffice. The only thing he could find that would hold fuel was an old bedpan. The grateful nun told him that the bedpan would work just fine. She carefully carried the gasoline back to her car, trying not to spill a drop. She got to her car and was slowly pouring the contents of the bedpan into the tank when a truck driver pulled alongside.

The truck driver rolled down his window and yelled to her, "I wish I had your faith, sister!"

"Good faith will last forever."

Psalm 40:1-8

He Lifted Me
Out of the Slimy Pit

Some people amaze me. They think if they just work hard enough, if they just have a positive attitude, if they redouble their efforts and run really fast, they will be able to distance themselves from all their problems. They're like a woman that Barbara Brown Taylor tells about.

Mrs. Taylor moved from the city out to the country. This woman, a friend of hers, came out for a visit. But, on the way, she got seriously lost. These were the days before cell phones and GPS, so she was on her own with nothing but some confusing directions and a badly out-of-date map. Already an hour later than she wanted to be, she was speeding through a small town of when she saw blue lights in her rearview mirror. Busted! She pulled over on the shoulder of the road and had her license ready when the officer arrived at her window.

"I am so sorry," she said, handing it to him along with her registration. "I know I was speeding, but I've been lost for the last forty minutes and I cannot find Tower Terrace anywhere on this map."

"Well, I'm sorry about that too, ma'am," the officer said, writing up her citation, "but what made you think that hurrying would help you find your way?"

Good question. We think if we work hard enough, if we redouble our efforts and just run fast enough, or if we have a positive attitude about everything, we can lift ourselves out of the slimy and desolate pit. Instead, we often dig a hole, deeper and more difficult to escape.

But it doesn't have to be that way. God is a God who rescues people from slimy pits. The Psalmist writes, *"I waited patiently for the Lord; he turned to me and heard my cry. He lifted me out of the slimy pit, out of the mud and mire; he set my feet on a rock and gave me a firm place to stand. He put a new song in my mouth, a hymn of praise to our God . . ."*

John 4:5-42

A Cake to Remember

A cake decorator was asked by a bride to inscribe the words from I John 4:18 on the wedding cake. I John 4:18 reads: *"There is no fear in love, but perfect love casts out fear."*

Unfortunately, the decorator got the instructions mixed up and instead of putting the words from I John 4:18 on the cake, the decorator wrote the words from the Gospel of John 4:18 on the cake. John 4:18 reads: *"You have had five husbands, and the man you now have is not your husband."*

The bride and groom did not see the cake until their reception, as they were getting ready to cut it! That bride had a lot of explaining to do.

A cake to remember!

Born on Christmas Day

It was two days before Christmas. There was a long line at the post office as people were trying frantically to use overnight mail to get Christmas packages to people on time. A woman with three little girls in tow finally reached the counter. "Can you get this package to Phoenix, Arizona by tomorrow?" she asked.

"I can, lady but it will cost you."

"How much?"

"Twenty-seven dollars and forty cents."

"My gracious," she said, "That's a lot, but I've got to do it. This present is for my father. It has to be there before Christmas because, you see, Christmas is also his birthday."

"Man! What a bummer that is!" said the postal clerk. "I sure am glad I don't know anyone who was born on Christmas Day."

Someone in the line spoke up. "I sure am glad I do !"

The Mystery of The Holy Trinity

It was said that a number of years ago a priest from The Church of the Annunciation on Anna Maria Island in Florida was walking along the beach when he came upon a young boy who kept filling a pail with sea water and pouring it on the sand.

The priest asked, "Son, what are you doing?"

The boy answered, "I'm emptying the Gulf of Mexico of all its water."

Laughing, the priest said, "I'm afraid that's impossible!"

The boy turned to the priest and asked, "And what are you doing, Father, walking here along the beach?"

The priest replied, "I am contemplating the mystery of the Holy Trinity."

The boy answered, "Father, I hate to tell you, but I'll empty the Gulf of Mexico before you fully understand the mystery of the Holy Trinity!"

Using Their Gifts

In the country of Sri Lanka, one of the poorest countries on earth, there is a small congregation with an unusual ministry. The congregation began taking the ministry of Jesus seriously. They began by praying and then asking, "What is there that we can do to meet the needs of hurting people around us that isn't being done by anyone else?"

After prayer, they found three significant needs. They discovered that many were so poor that had no way of getting their sick family members to the clinics. There were five cars within the membership of the church. Those cars have now been dedicated for ministry. They are being used for taking the poorest of the poor to and from the clinics.

Then they discovered a second thing. There were young women in their community who were to be married but they were too poor to buy a white wedding dress. So the ones who sewed used their gifts. The church now owns a number of beautiful white wedding dresses of various sizes. When a young woman comes to be married, she can wear one of those dresses.

A visitor to the church was amazed to see what was in a little tin-roofed shed located behind the church. It contained coffins of various sizes. He asked why there should be such a strange building filled with coffins behind the church, and discovered the third area of ministry in that congregation. He was told, "It is because our people are too poor to purchase coffins for their dead. Members of the church make the coffins for the poorest of the poor."

The builders of that church used their gifts. That congregation's experience of God is being translated into praise, service, and witness.

What other wonderful things could we be doing, what other needs could be met if we worked hard to find creative ways to further use our many God-given gifts and talents?

Matthew 17:1–9

Be Amazed

There is a cute story about a young man, let's call him Sam, who is having a conversation with God. It goes like this:

Sam: What is a million years to you, God?

God: Like a second.

Sam: What is a million dollars like to you?

God: Like a penny.

Sam: Wow! Can I have a penny?

God: Sure, just give me a second.

Let's give God more than a second of our time.

As we enter Lent, let us be like Peter, James and John who were amazed by the wonder of the Transfiguration and were never again the same.

John 4:5–42
Truly, Living Water

While I was in seminary, I received a grant to go to Nairobi, Kenya for a summer. We were to be enrolled in a college and identify a thesis to work on. Mine was on traditional and modern medicine of Africa.

I had no idea that I would find a place of such poverty and true scarcity of water. It was not like anything we know. A water shortage in America means not to water your lawn or wash your car on Tuesdays or Thursdays. This does not compare to what I experienced in Africa.

Each day, we were given a small plastic margarine tub of water. That was our day's water for our personal needs. There was no water in the bathrooms. We were given bottled water to drink . . . but not much.

On our bus ride to the college, we would pass lines of Africans with their water jugs, getting water for cooking and bathing for the entire family. Most of their days were spent in hours of walking to the village well, drawing water for the family, balancing the earthen jar on their heads and walking back to their homes. They would repeat this each and every day.

Actually, when I returned home to New Haven, I had a difficult time spending more than two minutes in the shower. How easily we take water for granted. In our part of the world all we need to do is turn a faucet and out it comes - clean, safe, drinkable, life-giving water. If only all the people in the world had that privilege.

Let us be truly thankful for all that we have.

John 4:5-42

Showing by Life and Example

In Bruce Larsen's book, *Ask Me to Dance*, there is the story of a member of his congregation who had come from another country.

Rev. Larsen said of this person, "Her faith sparkled and the living water of the spirit flowed out of her soul to all around her."

He invited her to go with him to a seminar on the topic of evangelism. The leaders had prepared tables filled with all sorts of pamphlets and strategies and demographic studies, all aimed at reaching the un-churched in their area. At some point during the program, the leaders turned to this woman and asked her to share some of the reasons that made the church so important and so vital in her home country.

At first she was a bit intimidated by the crowds, but then she said: "Well, we never give pamphlets to people. We don't even have them. We just show people by our life and example what it is like to be a Christian, and when they can see for themselves, then they want to be a Christian, too."

That's is what we are to do. Show people by our life and example what it is like to be a Christian. And our not only our lives but other lives will be changed!

Remembering 9/11

It has been a number of years since we watched two hours of terrorism unfold before our eyes. We will always remember where we were and what we were doing on that day.

I will never forget that day. I was in charge of reassembling the children's chapel at St. Thomas Episcopal School. We had just completed the regular chapel one hour earlier where we were responding to a death of one of the school children's mother. We again met with the 240 children, telling them about the 9/11 tragedy, yet assuring them that they were safe. And then later we spent hours with parents processing the utter disbelief, anger and fear.

I remember back to September 2011. I had been thinking about the effects of September 11th on those children and all children on this the tenth anniversary of the terrorist attack. I was at the grocery store check-out lane and the *People* magazine caught my eye. On the cover was the picture of a beautiful young lady, nine years of age. The lead article featured the children who were in the wombs of the mothers as their fathers died on September 11, 2001. Their fathers died on September 11th, after they had been conceived, but before any of them were born. I thought, "Where is the hope for these children?"

One of those children named Alexa wrote: "I always ask my mom to see pictures of my dad and me, but then I remember there aren't any. That makes me sad. My dad was a firefighter who died when the Twin Towers fell. I don't like listening to the story of what happened to my dad. I know it was his job, but sometimes I wish on that day he wasn't so brave. I know that my Dad was wonderful. My Dad gave me hope. When I see the people running from the building that day, I know my Dad was telling them to get out. And that makes me proud."

Each of the ten children in the article were victims of 9/11 for their fathers died on that day. There was no father there for them when they were born. Yet Grace, Rodney, Alexa, Parker, Lauren, Ronald, Robyn, Jamie, Allison, and Gabriel embrace life with amazing grace. The love of God has sustained their mothers to believe in hope and faith and to instill that love of God in these beautiful boys and girls.

Ten-year-old Robyn wrote: "A few years ago, I started reading the Pledge of Allegiance at our towns' memorial service on 9/11. I like people knowing that I am growing up being part of history. My friends at school help me. My best friend sat next to me at the lunch table on 9/11 and we looked at my necklace, which has a picture of my dad on it. Oh, how I would have loved to have known my Dad."

September 11th. I know some of you are thinking . . . "Oh great, why does the anniversary have to fall on a Sunday? Why do we have to be reminded that there were people just going to work on a typical day and they never came home? Why do we have to remember that the violence that happened was on U.S. soil? Why do we have to be reminded of these things?"

Why? Because it is a reminder of the hurt, the loss, the pain. It is a reminder that there is evil in the world. But more than that, as hard as it may be, it is also a reminder of the need for love and forgiveness.

Let's Bake Some Bread

When the Holy Spirit is experienced, people walk with courage and confidence. No one needs to ask, "Can we do this, dare we try that?" Nothing is impossible to people who are led by the Spirit. And it is powerful.

It is like the time when a husband thought he would surprise his family and bake some fresh bread. He consulted with his wife who told him where to find the recipe. He went to the kitchen counter and carefully assembled the flour, shortening, milk, yeast, etc.

But somehow a portion of the recipe sheet had been torn off and the correct amount of yeast was missing. He wanted to make sure he added enough yeast so he added several packets, many times more than would have been called for in the recipe. "No problem if I add too much," he reasoned, "If a little yeast is good, a lot of yeast will be better."

A little later his wife called downstairs, "Honey, have you put the bread in the oven yet?"

The distraught husband yelled from the kitchen, "Put it in the oven? I can't even keep it in the kitchen!"

The bread had taken a life of its own . . . had its own power.

It is Pentecost! Let's bake some bread.

We Are So Privileged, We Sometimes Forget

We are so privileged - we have so much. We sometimes forget how little many other people in this world have.

John Bowes, the one-time chairman of the parent company of Wham-O, the maker of Frisbees, once participated in a charity effort. He sent thousands of the plastic flying discs to an orphanage in Angola, Africa. He thought the children there would enjoy playing with them.

Several months later, a representative from the company visited the orphanage. One of the nuns thanked him for the wonderful *plates* that his company had sent them. She told him the children were eating off the *plates,* carrying water with them, and even catching fish with them. When the representative explained how the Frisbees were intended to be used, the nun was even more delighted that the children would now also be able to enjoy them as toys.

On one level, that story is rather amusing. On another, it is very sad. There are people who would prize even our cast-off items, who would be grateful to eat what we throw away. To have just a cup of cold water.

An Act of True Love

A number of years ago, in San Antonio, Texas, a fifth-grade teacher gave a homework assignment for Valentine's Day. The subject was true love. The students were to return the next day with a true story of how they had either expressed love, or had received love, or had witnessed an act of true love.

The next day, when it was Kassi's turn to address the class, she told this story:

"My mom and I drove to McDonald's for lunch last week and as we pulled into the parking lot we noticed a homeless man and a mangy dog sitting on the curb next to the street.

"My mom didn't say anything to me but I noticed as she placed our order she ordered an extra Quarter Pounder with cheese. As we were leaving the restaurant and heading to our car she walked over to the homeless man and handed him the bag with the extra hamburger she had ordered."

"That's a wonderful story, Kassi," said the teacher. "And that was certainly an expression of love."

"No, no," replied Kassi, "that's not my example of love."

"Oh," said the teacher. "I don't understand. What was the example of love?"

Kassi ended the conversation by saying, "It was when we were driving out of the parking lot and saw the homeless man tearing the hamburger apart and giving half of it to his dog."

Mark 6:30–34, 53–56

He Will Meet You

God's compassionate love is good news for us because we are often like the people Jesus touched - the fallen, the blind, the deaf, the sinners, the lost, the least, the despised, the unloved. We are those people.

A little first-grader hurried into the classroom and said, "Teacher, two boys are fighting on the playground, and I think the one on the bottom wants you."

We feel like that often. We sometimes feel life gets us down. God has sent Jesus Christ to rescue us - to show us the way, to help us, to meet us, to lead us.

An old rabbi told a story of a boy who ran away from home. He was one-hundred days' journey away. He sent his father a message that he wanted to come home, but he did not think he could make it.

His father sent him a message back: "Go as far as you can, and I will come the rest of the way to meet you."

A Christmas Story

"Well, Now, This is Fixable"

One day very close to Christmas, a young boy named Landon was coming down the hallway at church. He had in his hand a little ceramic dish that he had made in Sunday School. It was to be his Christmas gift to his mother. He had been working on it for several weeks and was so proud of it.

As Landon ran down the hall, he tripped and fell. The dish crashed to the floor and broke into several pieces. The little boy was devastated. He began to cry loudly and uncontrollably. He was absolutely heartbroken.

People tried to comfort him with all kinds of counsel: "Everything will be alright." "It was just a dish; You can make another one." "You can make your mother something else." But nothing helped. The child was inconsolable.

Just then his grandmother arrived on the scene. Quickly she realized what had happened.

Kneeling down beside her devastated and distraught grandson with his broken gift, she hugged him tightly and said, "Well, now, I think this is fixable. Let's pick up the pieces and take it all home. We'll put it back together and see what we can make of it. Your mother will be so happy with your gift."

The little boy hugged his grandmother back and smiled.

Isn't that exactly what the Christmas message is about? The world is broken into many fragments, as are our lives.

And God stoops down beside us. He hugs us and says, "Well, now, this is fixable. Let me help you pick up the pieces. We'll put it back together and see what we can make of it."

You Will Never Be Lost

The six-year-old twin brother and sister knew they were not to go wandering off from home alone, but the lure of the nearby candy store was too strong to resist.

Perhaps due to the candy-induced sugar-high, upon leaving the candy store they headed off in the wrong direction and soon found themselves on an unfamiliar street and lost.

They ran up and down the adjoining streets, but didn't recognize any of the houses.

Of course, they became very frightened and scared and started to cry. Some people tried to help and comfort them, and then called the police.

Soon a policeman arrived to help them. He called the department to find out if anyone was calling for the children and then put them in the patrol car to bring them to the police department until they could find their parents.

As they were driving, the little girl saw their church and said to the policeman, "Wait. Stop. This is our church. You can let us out; we know our way home from here."

Be like that little girl and boy. Let the church be the starting place to find anything in your life. Make the church a familiar place to come, to pray, to share, and to listen to God. Come here often. Not just on Sundays.

And if you do, you will never be lost. You will be a child of God.

Matthew 28:16-20
"I Am With You Always."

In this gospel, and the Gospel of Mark, ends with this profound statement from Jesus to his disciples: *"And remember, I am with you always, to the end of the age."*
This is our assurance that no matter how downtrodden, no matter how depressed, no matter how lonely, no matter how ill, no matter how scarred you might feel, God will be there with you. Believe in that.

In 1989, an 8.2 earthquake almost flattened Armenia, killing over 30,000 people in less than four minutes. In the midst of utter devastation and chaos, a father left his wife securely at home and rushed to the school where his 14-year-old son was supposed to be, only to discover that the building was as flat as a pancake.

After the traumatic initial shock, he remembered the promise he had made to his son: "No matter what, I'll always be there for you!"

He began to concentrate on where his son's classroom was located. Remembering the classroom would be in the back right corner of the building, he rushed there and started digging through the rubble.

As he was digging, other forlorn parents arrived, clutching their hearts, saying: "My son! My daughter!" After digging for several hours some of the parents tried to pull him off of what was left of the school saying: "It's too late! They're dead!" "Face reality, there's nothing you can do, you're just going to make things worse!"

To each parent, he responded, "Are you going to help me?" But none did. He continued to dig for his son, stone by stone.

The fire chief showed up and tried to pull him off of the debris shouting, "Fires are breaking out, explosions are happening everywhere. You're in danger. We'll take care of this. Go home." To which the Armenian father asked, "Are you going to help me?"

The police came and said, "You're angry, distraught and it's over. You're endangering others. Go home. We'll handle it!" To which he replied, "Are you going to help me?" Again, no one helped.

Courageously he proceeded alone thinking, "Is my son alive or is he dead?" He dug for eight hours . . . twelve hours . . . 24 hours . . . and then, in the 28th hour, he pulled back a boulder and heard his son's voice. He screamed his son's name, "Armand!"

He heard back, "Dad? It's me, Dad! I told the other kids not to worry. You promised that no matter what you would always be there for me!"

"Are you hurt? Is everyone OK?" the father asked.

"There are twelve of us left out of the thirty-three in my class, Dad. We're scared, hungry, thirsty, and very, very happy you are here. When the building collapsed, it made a wedge, like a triangle, and it saved us."

"Here, grab my hand. Come on out, son!"

"No, Dad. Let the other kids out first, I told them that if you were alive you'd save me and when you saved me, they'd be saved. I know you'll get me! No matter what, I know you'll always be there for me!"

And Jesus said, "*And remember, I am with you always, to the end of the age.*"

Your Story:

With Christ in your life, your story will not only be a good one, it will be a GREAT ONE!

AMEN!

The Rev. Dee Ann de Montmollin

The Rev. de Montmollin is a graduate of Yale Divinity School and Berkeley at Yale Episcopal Seminary. She was ordained in the Diocese of Southeast Florida and served as Assistant Rector at St. Thomas Episcopal Church in Coral Gables, FL. She was then called as Rector of St. Francis Episcopal Church in Rutherfordton, NC, where she served for seven years. In order to live closer to their grandchildren, she then accepted a call to be Rector of The Episcopal Church of the Annunciation on Anna Maria Island, FL.

Following five years at Annunciation, she felt motivated by the Holy Spirit to move to other ministries. In 2015, she retired from active parish ministry and now divides her time between medical mission trips, leading retreats, and providing individual spiritual direction.

In addition to her Masters of Divinity degree, she also holds an undergraduate degree in Behavioral Science and a Masters Degree in Mental Health Counseling. She holds Florida licensures as a Mental Health Counselor and as a Registered Nurse. Prior to entering seminary she was Executive Director of the Samaritan Counseling Center for the Diocese of Southeast Florida and a member of the Psycho-Oncology team at Sylvester Cancer at the University of Miami. She is also a graduate of the Shalem Institute for Spiritual Formation in Baltimore.

The Rev. de Montmollin offers personalized individual and small group retreats on Anna Maria Island in Florida and in the mountains of Western North Carolina. For additional information, email her at **revdee1@frontier.com**.

Made in the USA
Charleston, SC
28 April 2016